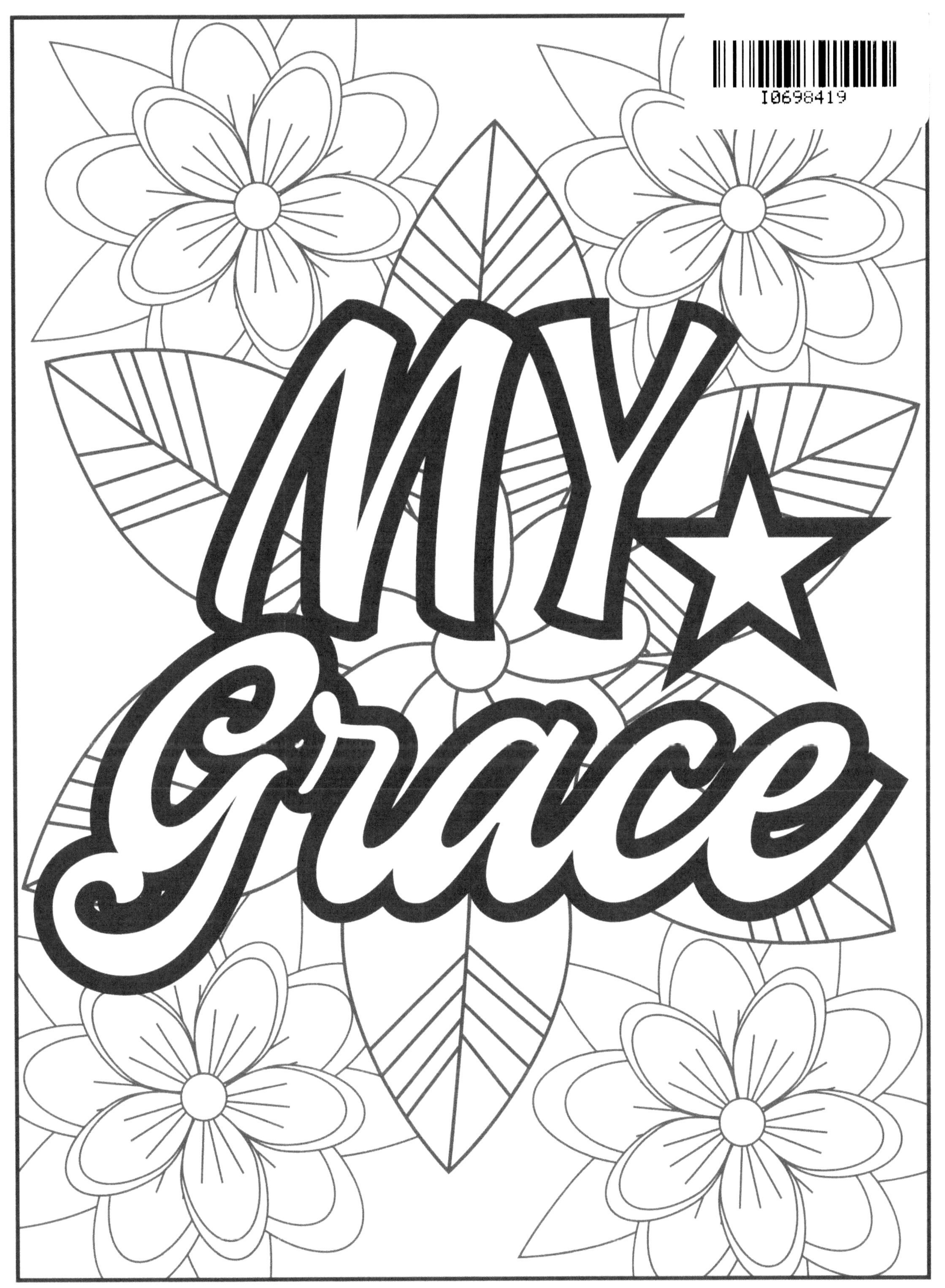

MY
Grace

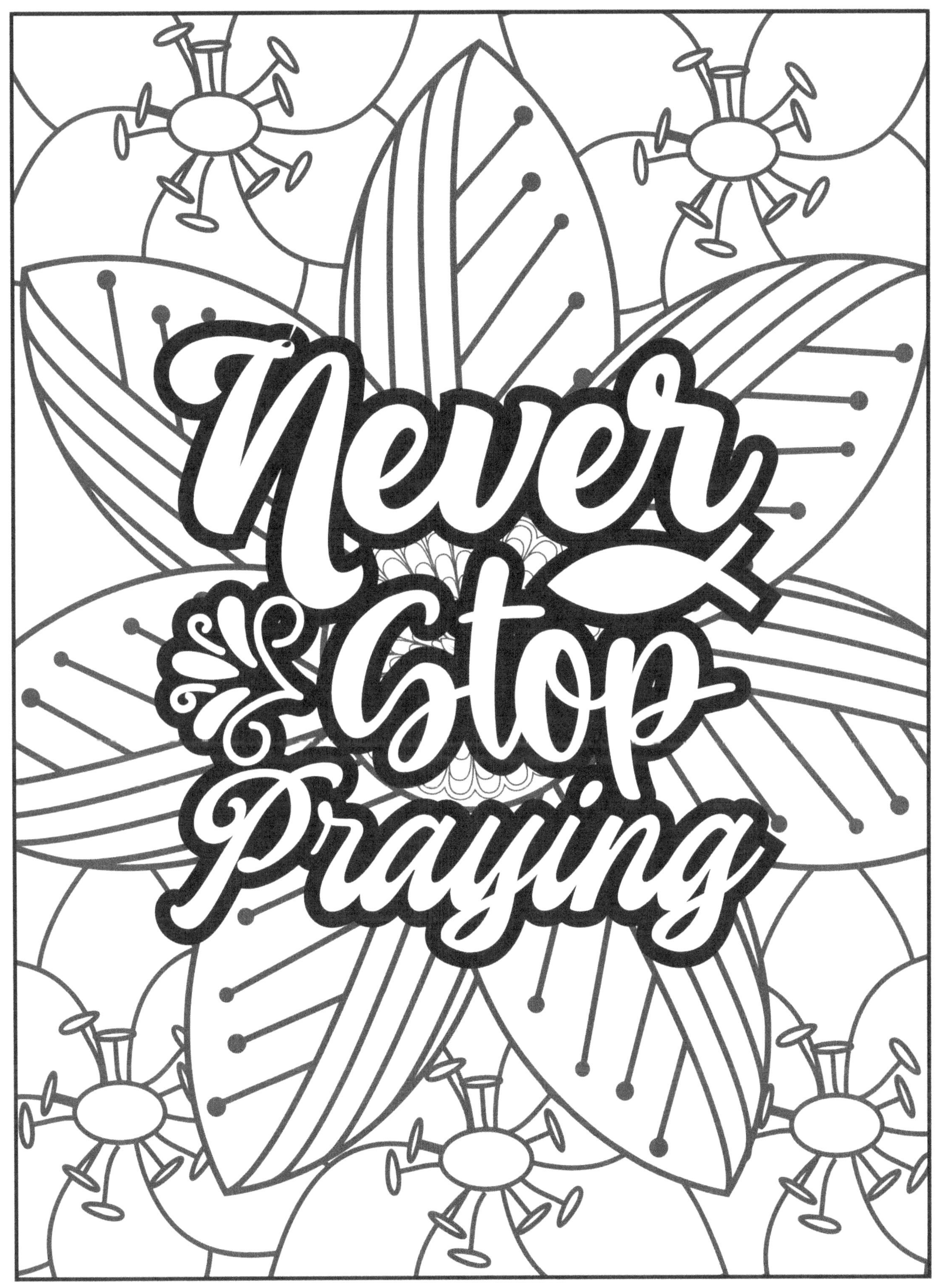

Never
Stop
Praying

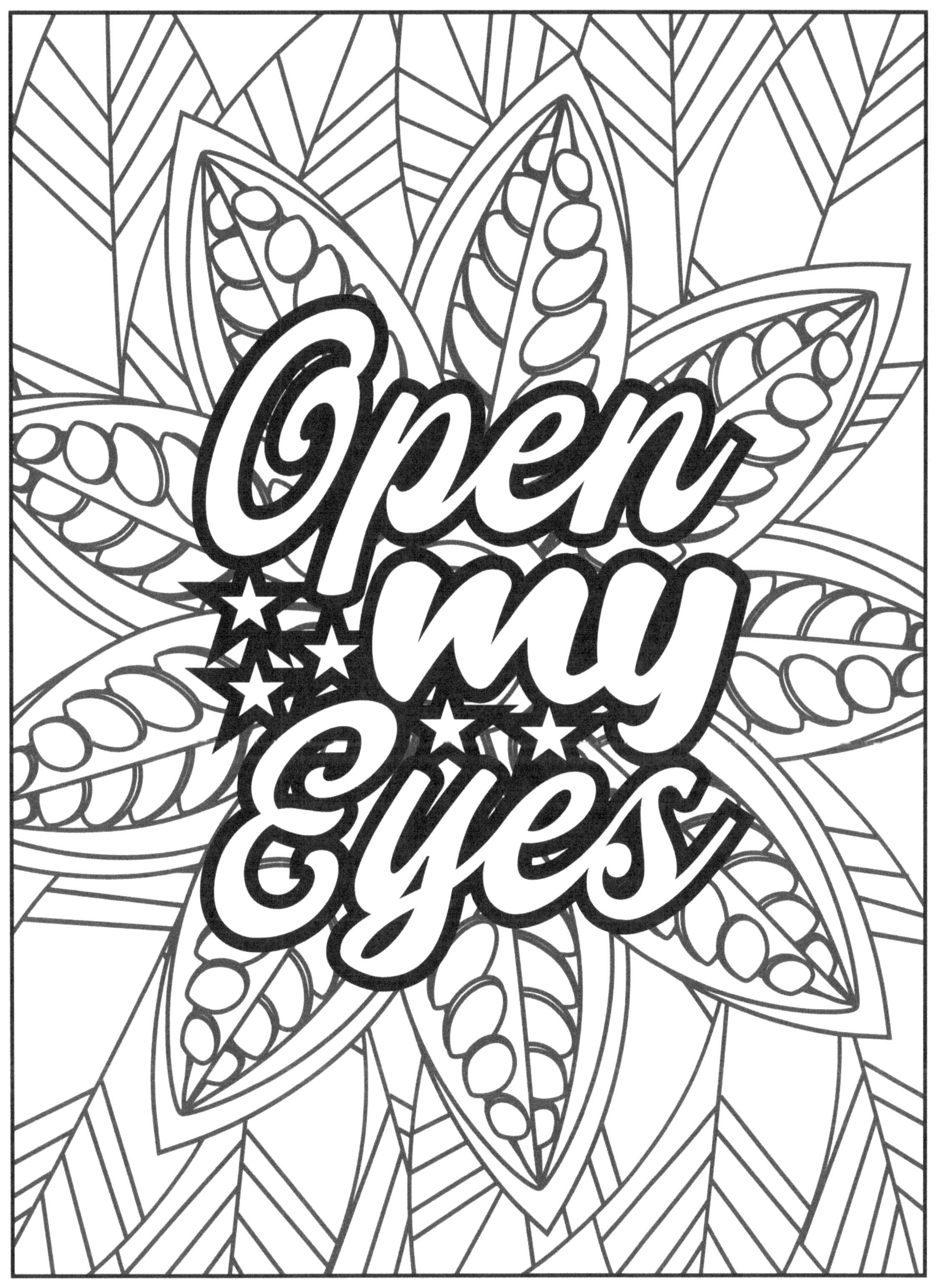
Open my Eyes

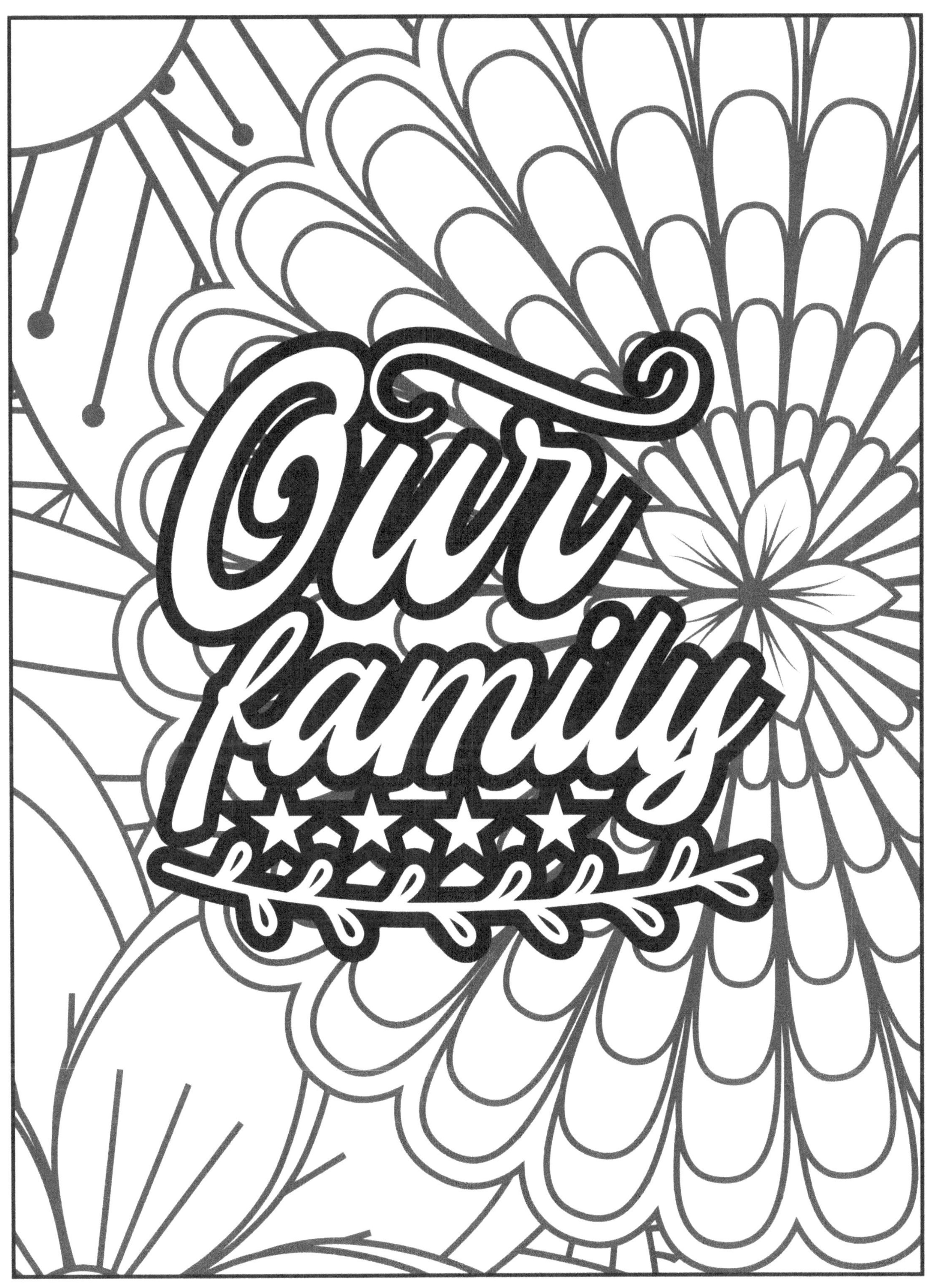
Our family

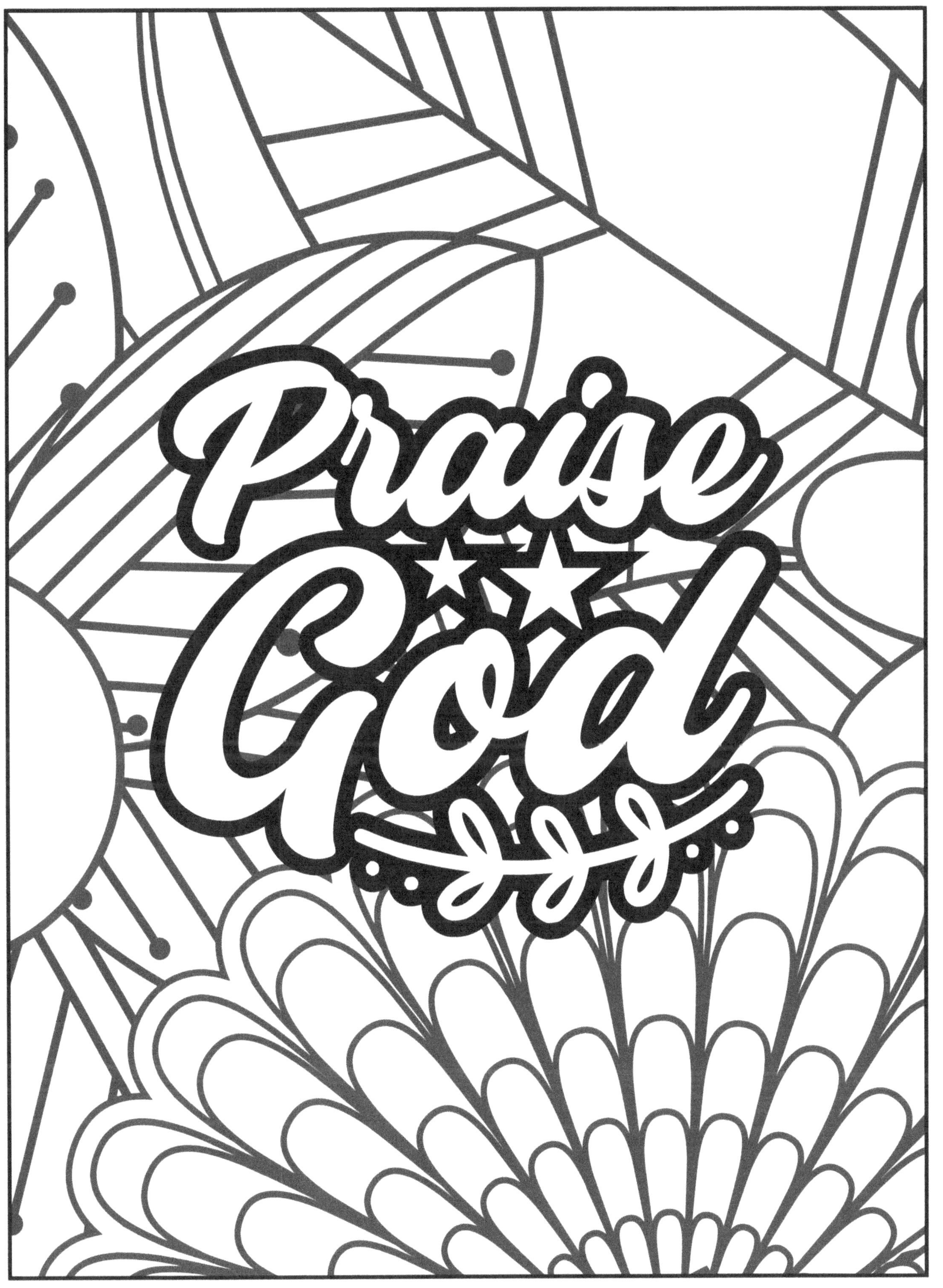

Praise
God

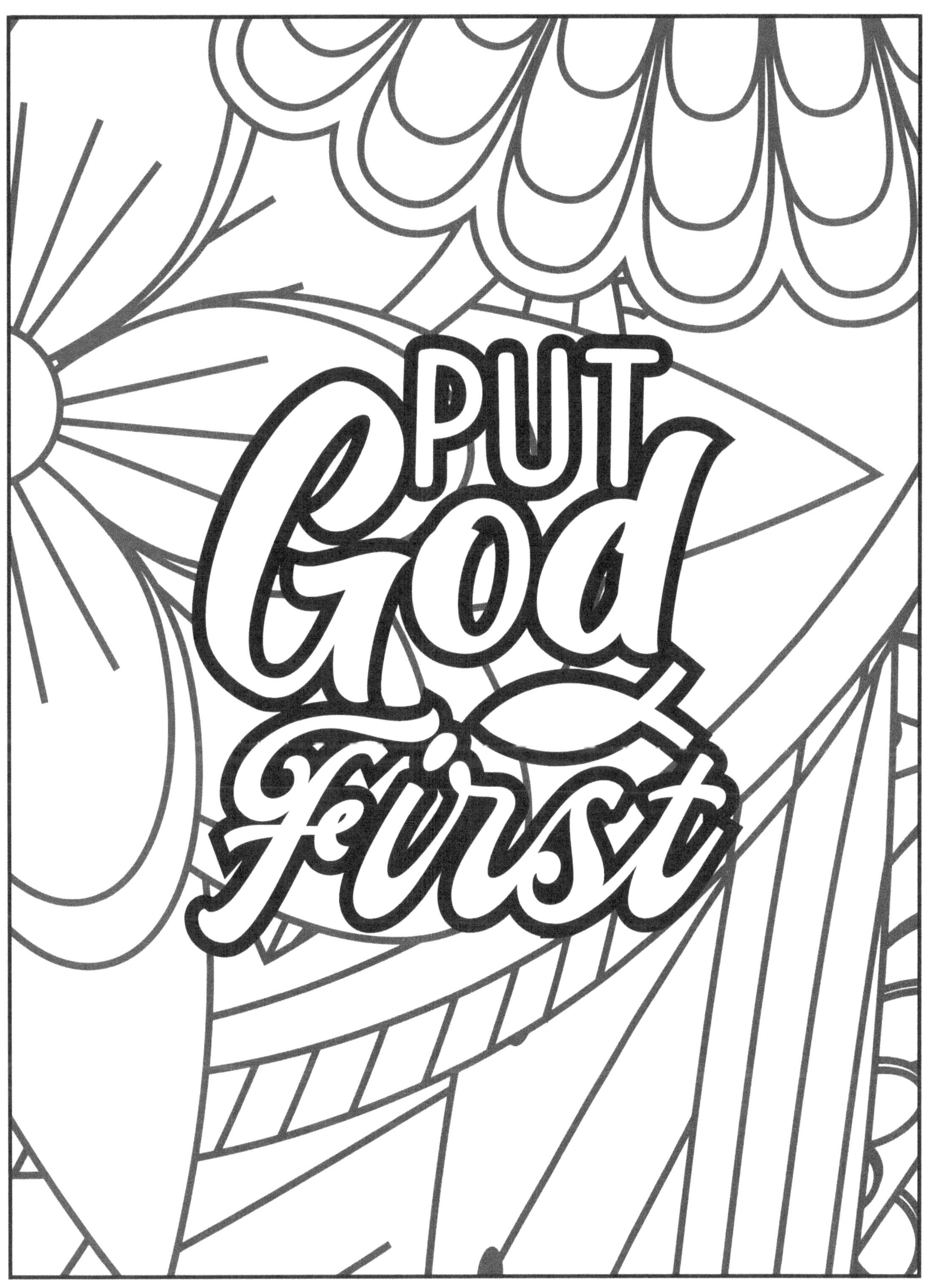

PUT
God
First

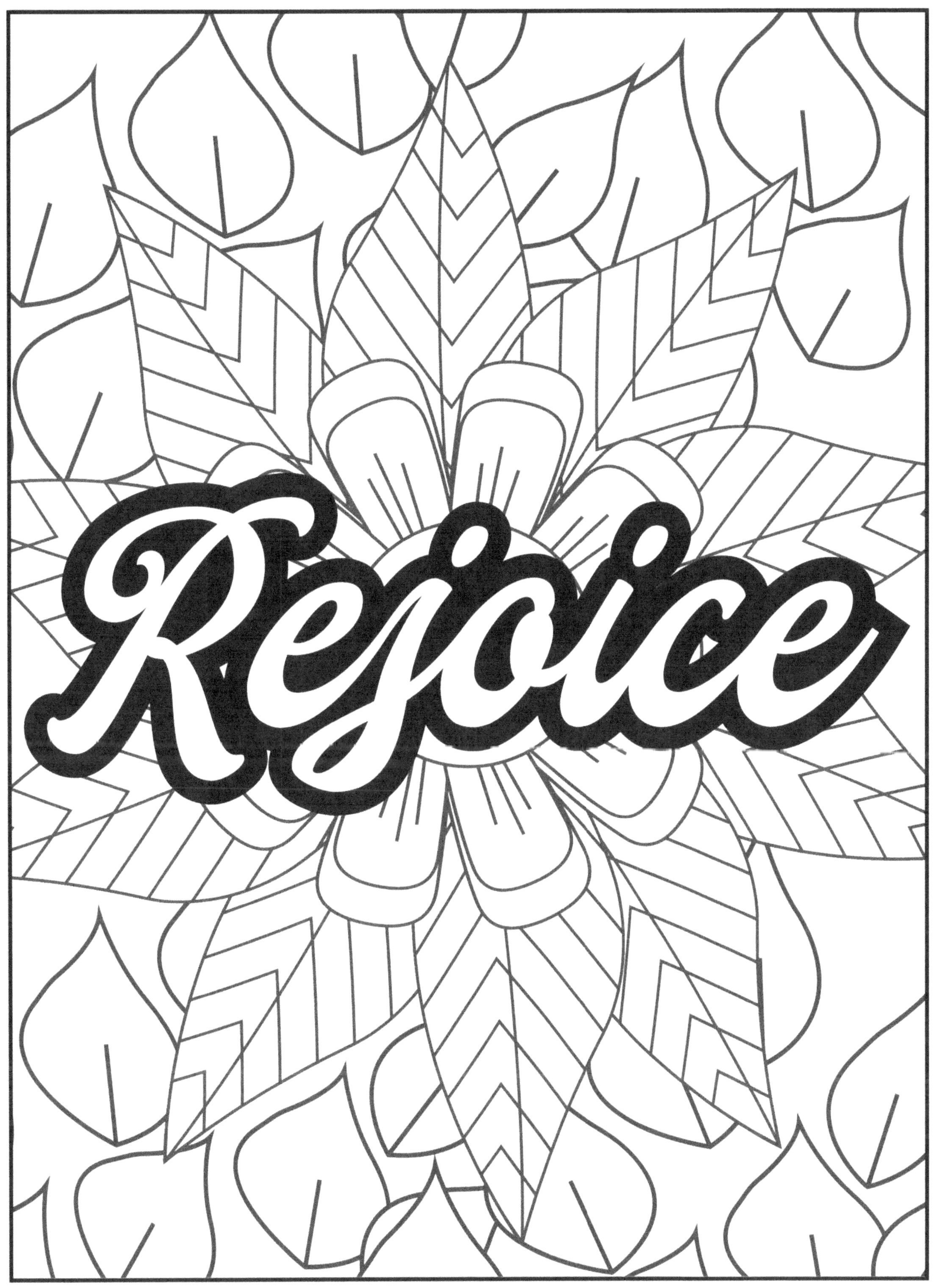
Rejoice

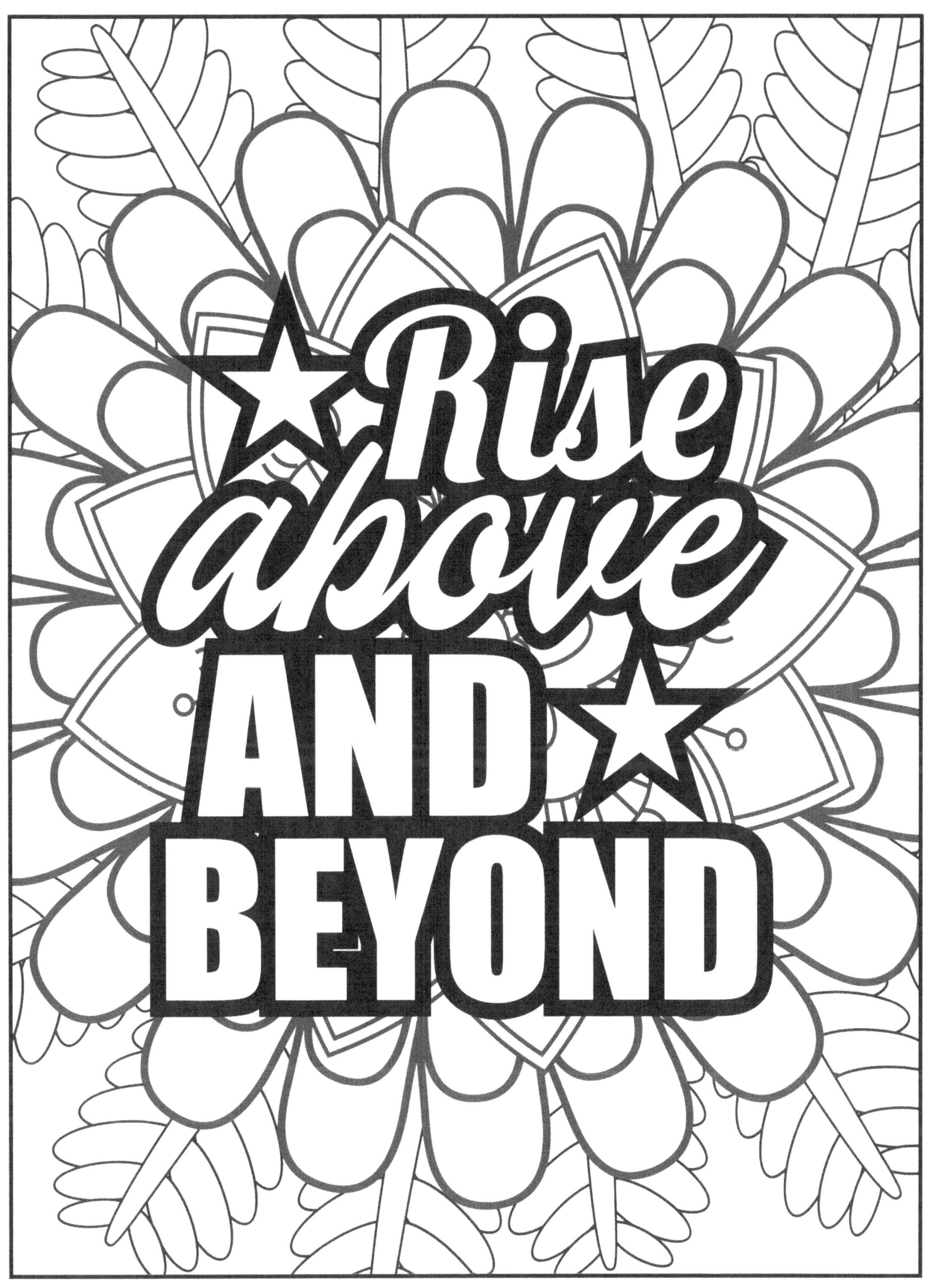

Rise above
AND
BEYOND

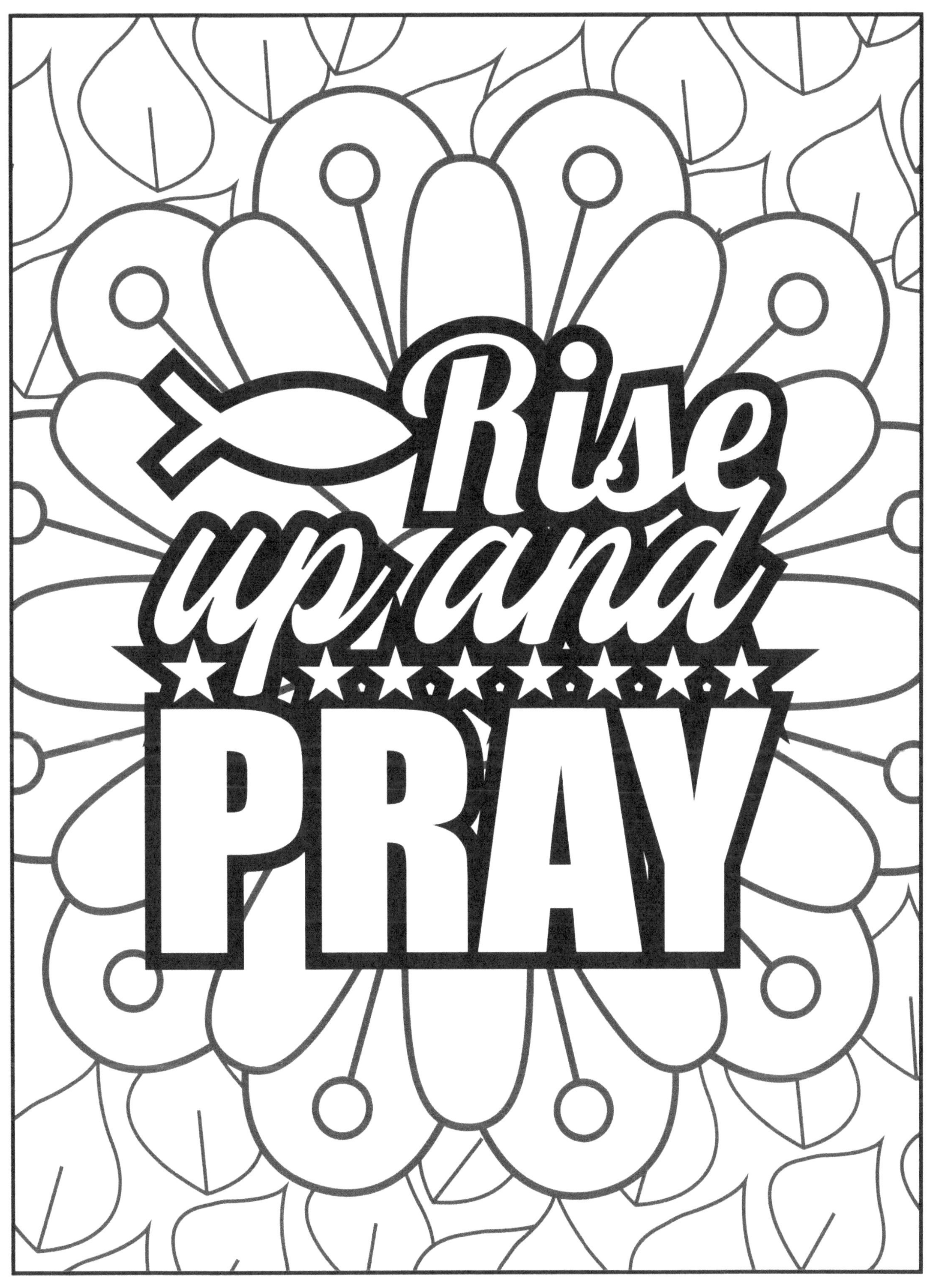

Rise up and
PRAY

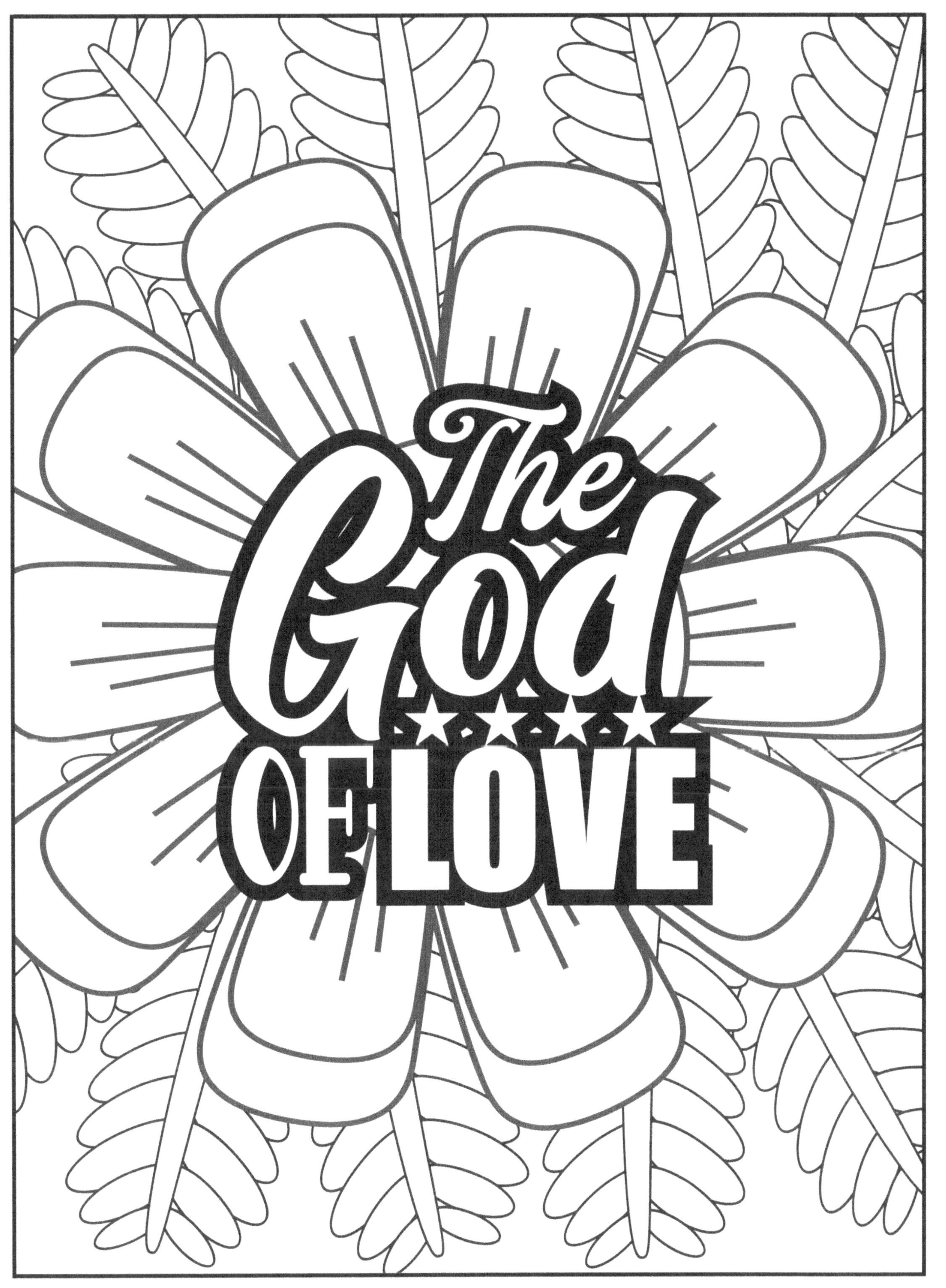

The
God
OF LOVE

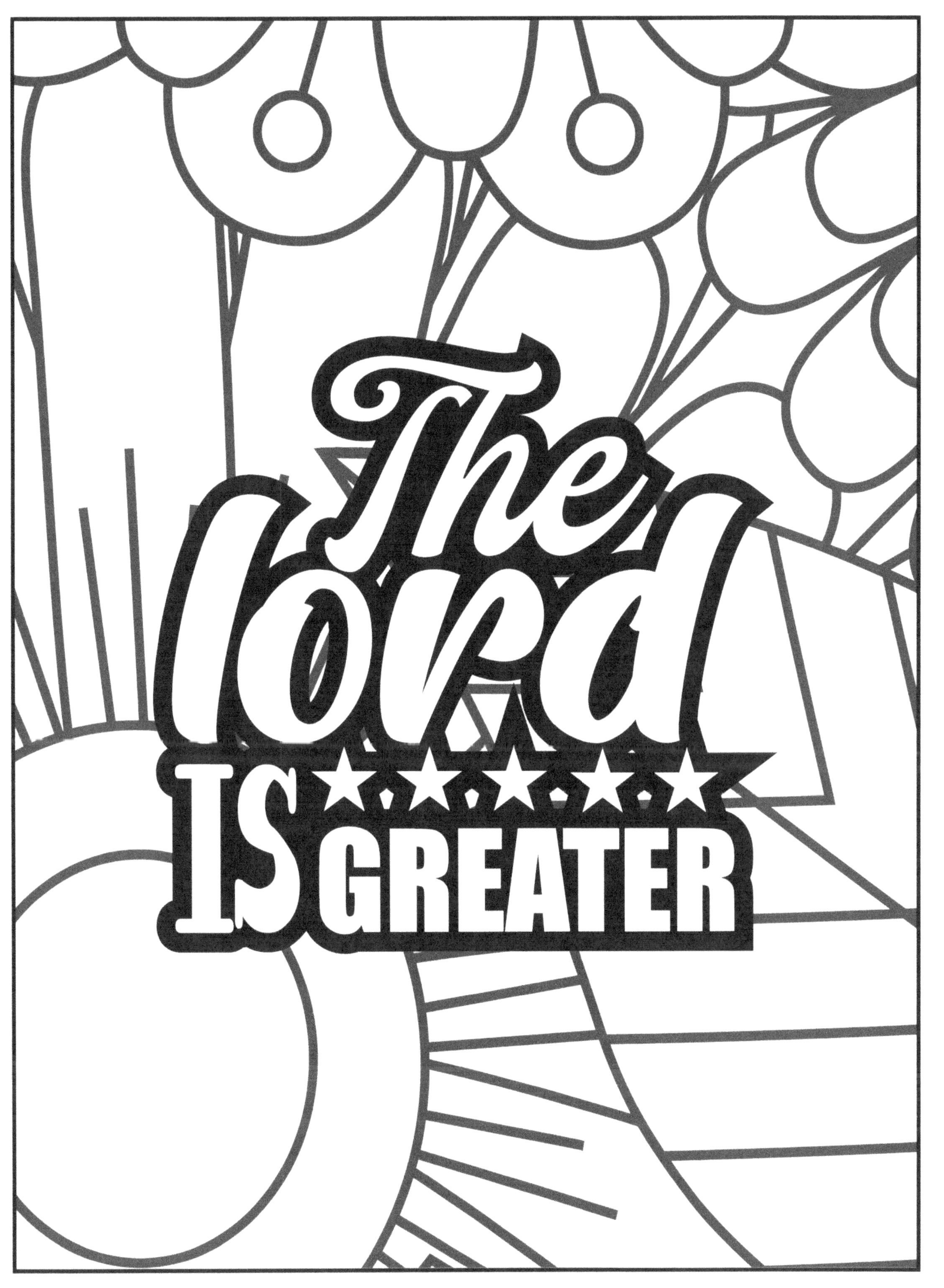

The Lord
IS GREATER

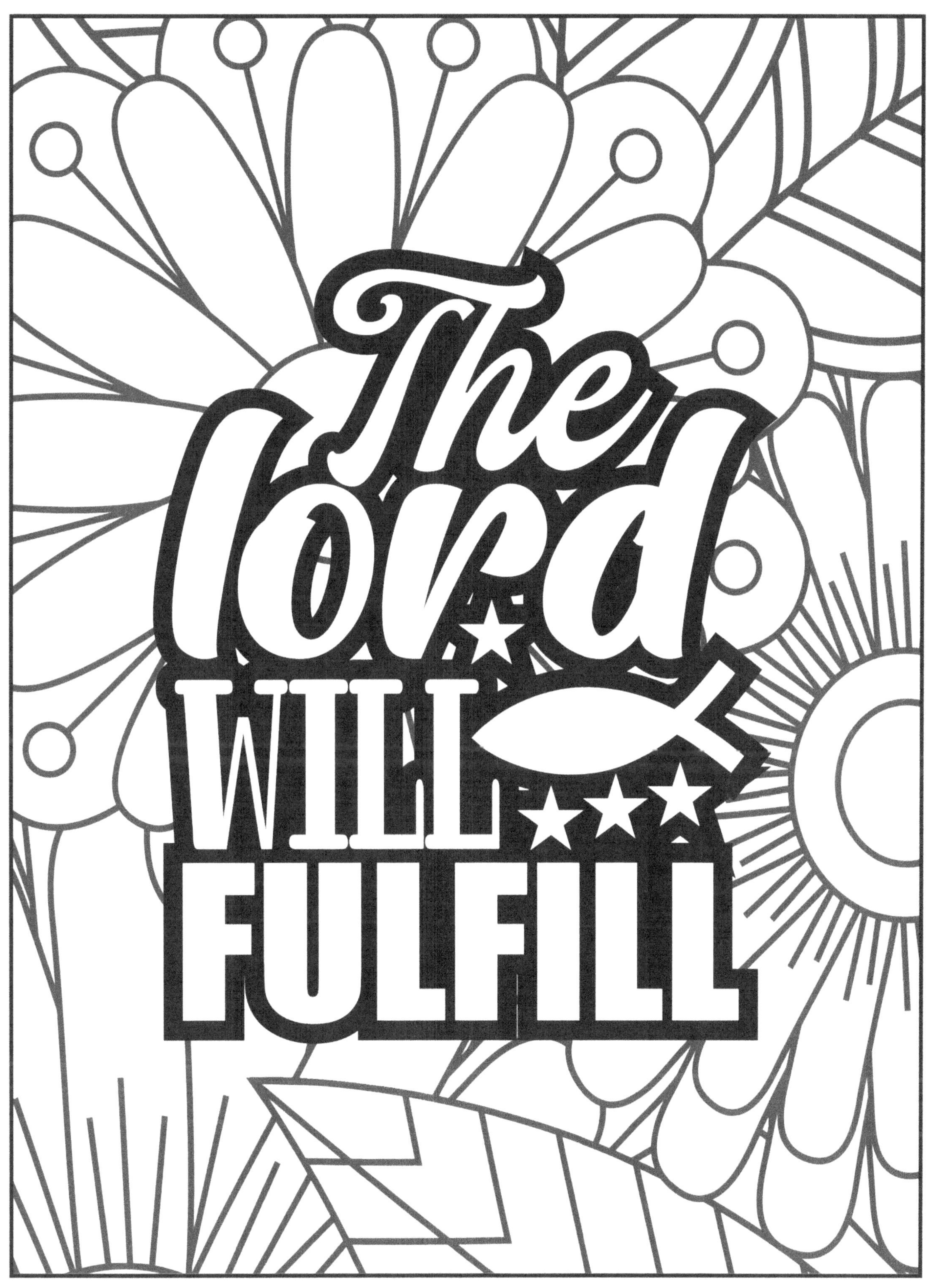

The Lord
will
fulfill

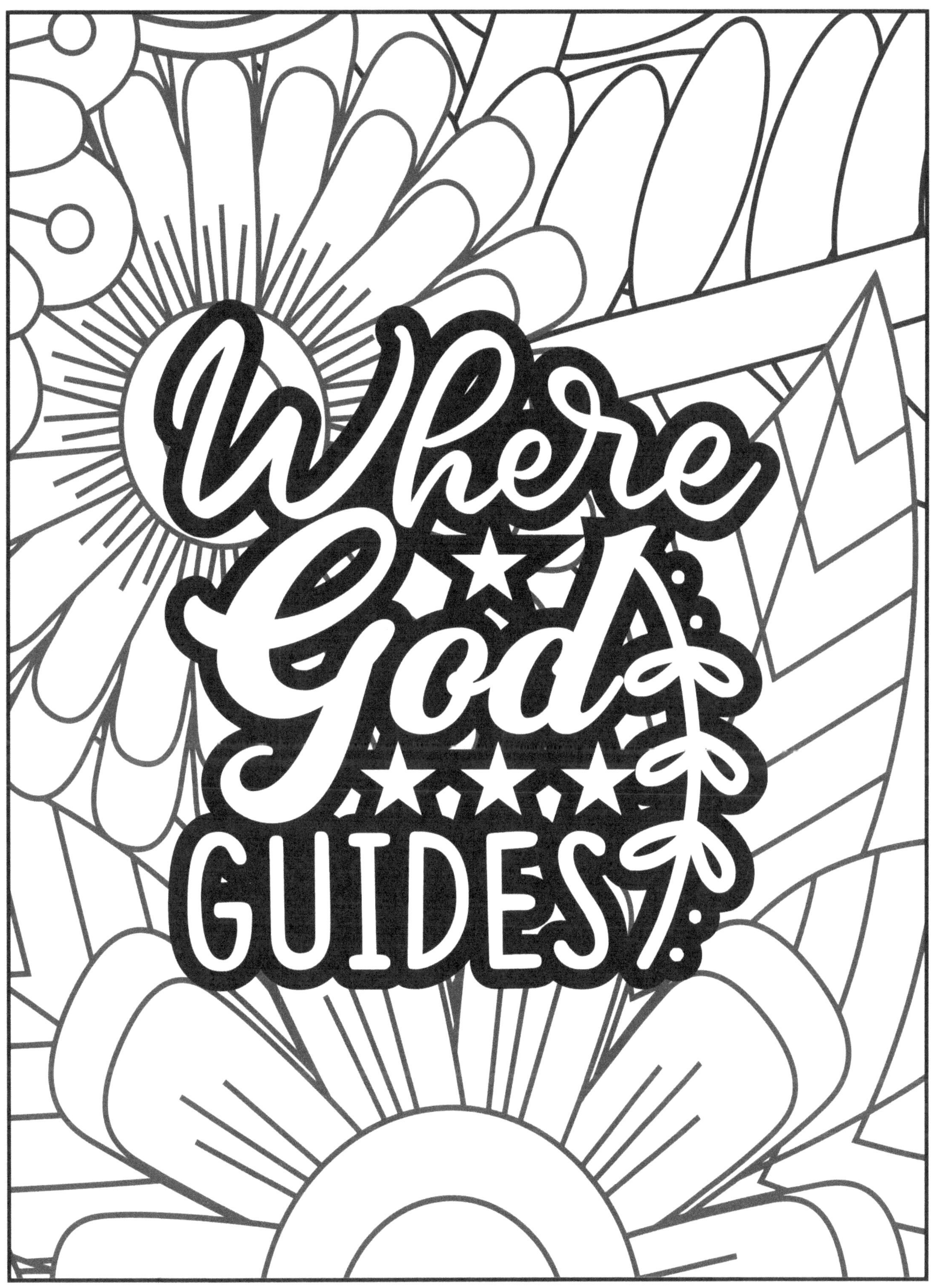

Where
God
GUIDES.

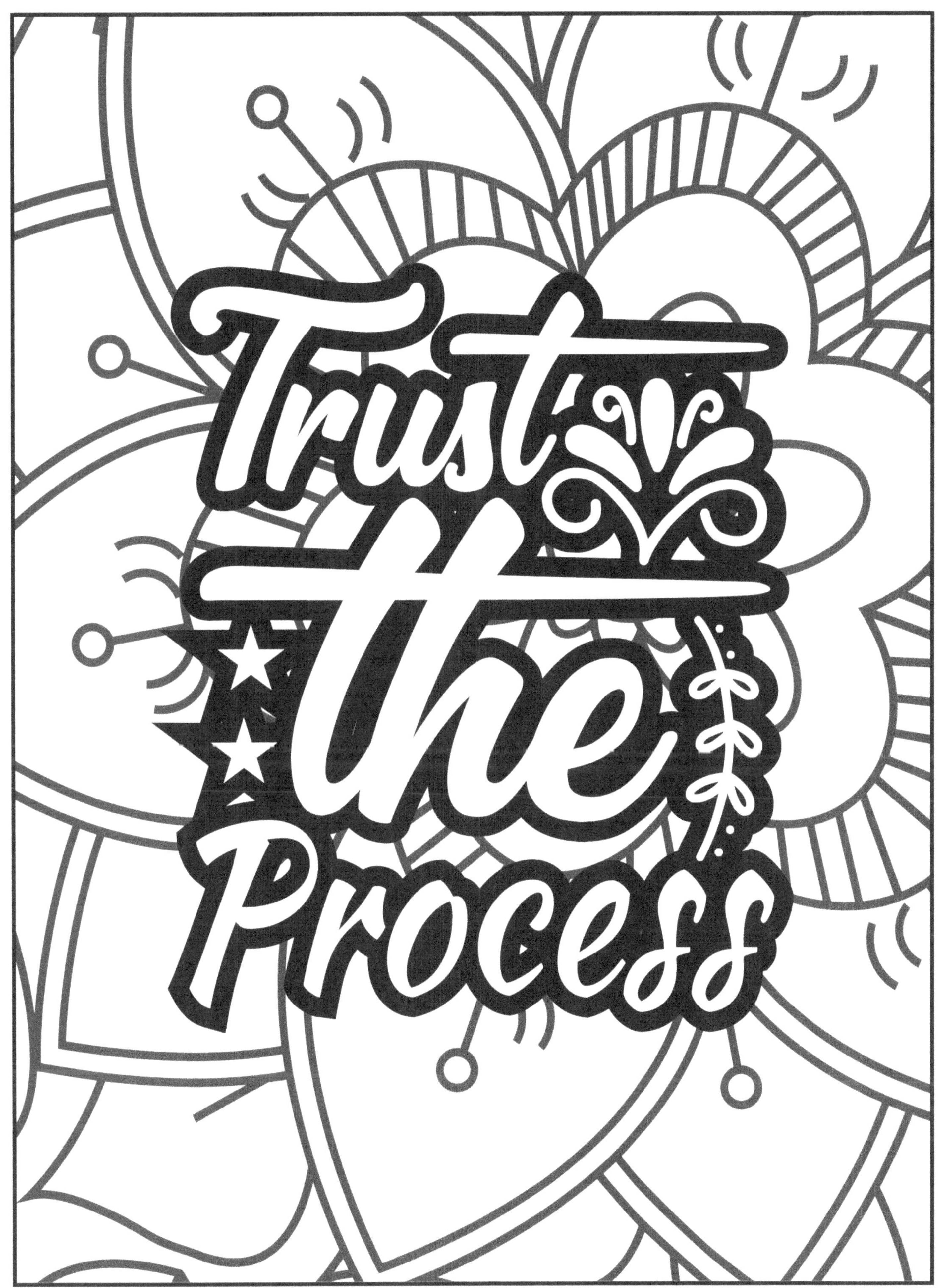

Trust
the
Process

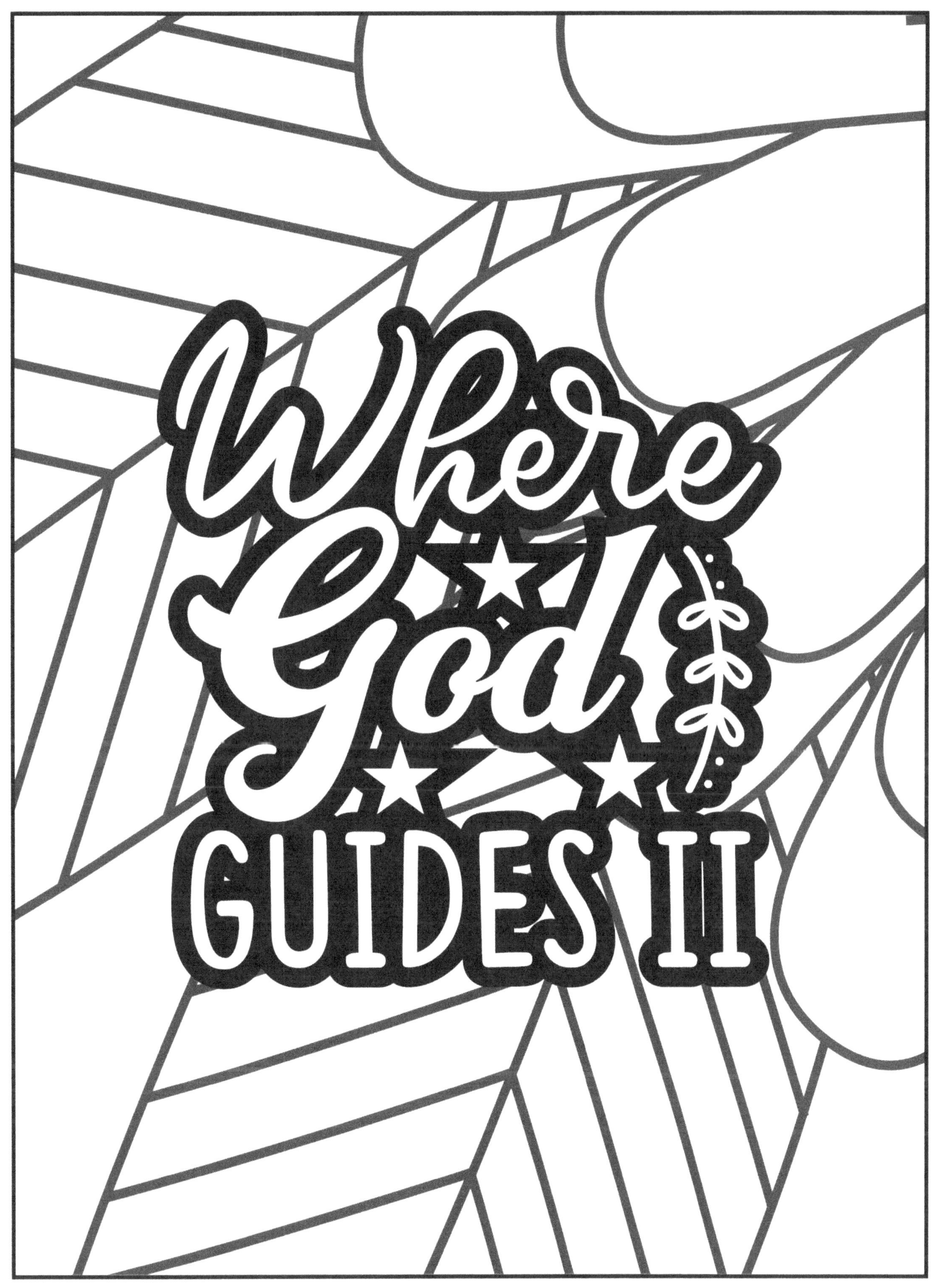

Where
God
GUIDES II

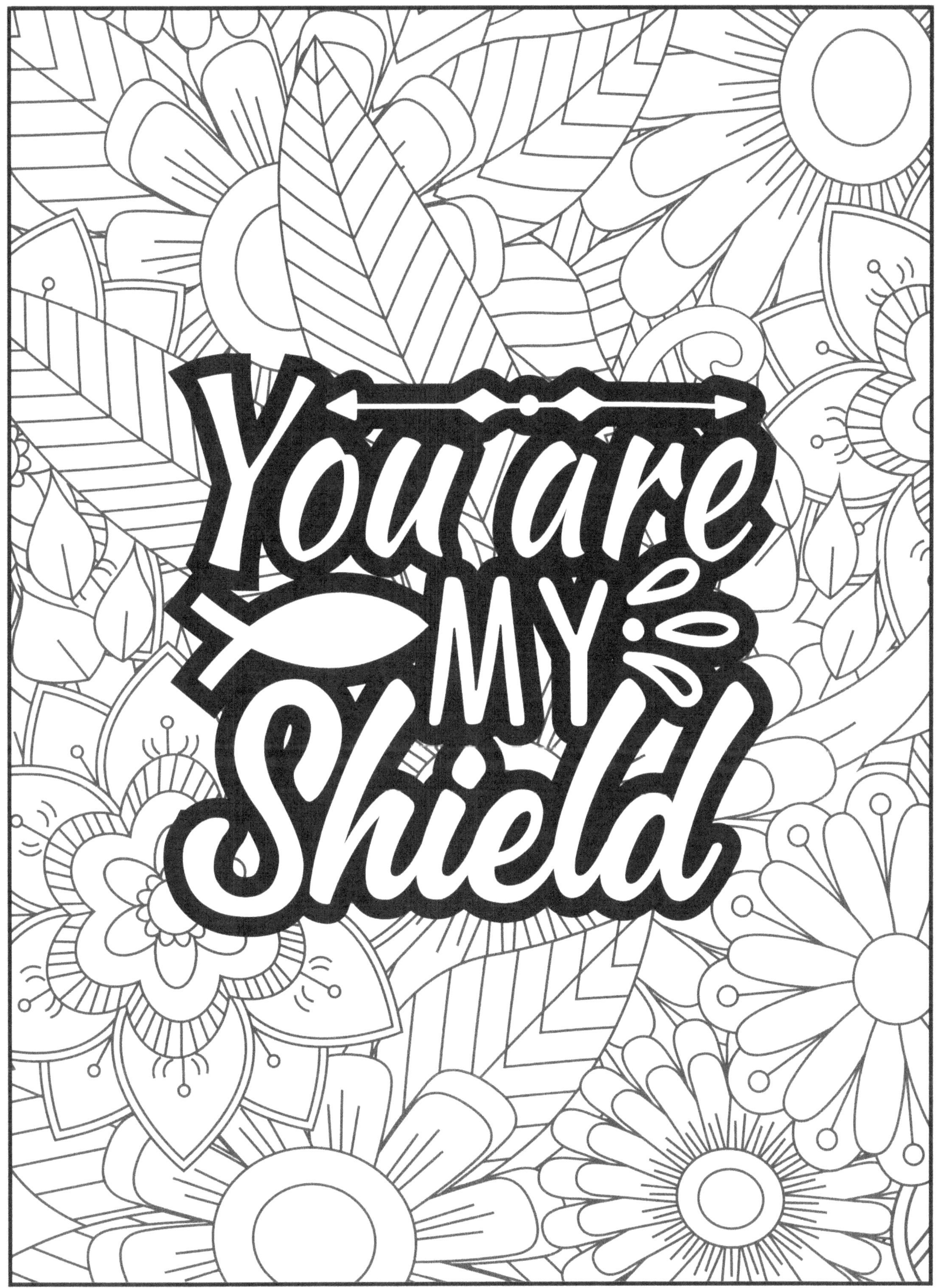

You are
MY
Shield

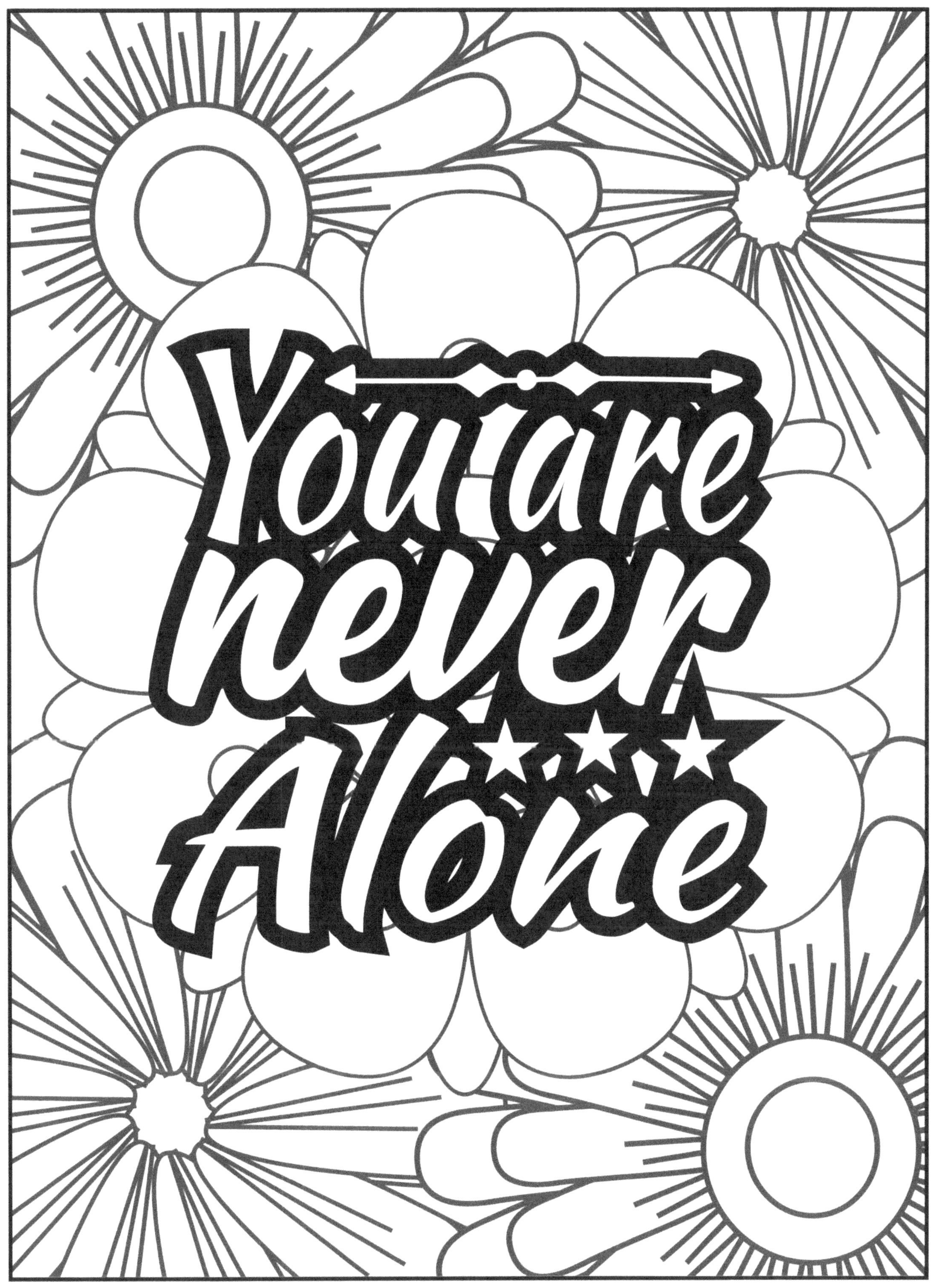

You are
never
Alone

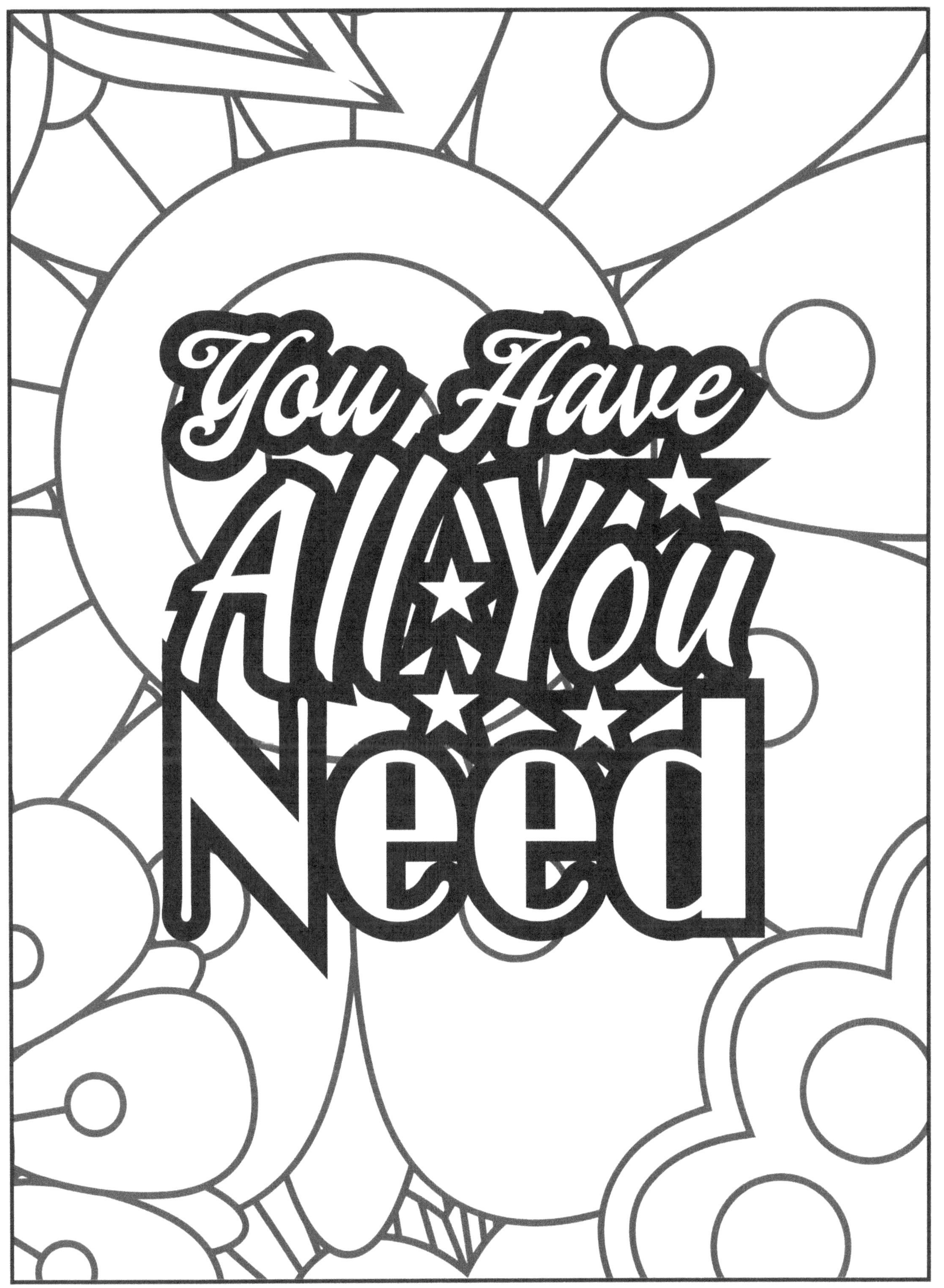

You Have
All You
Need

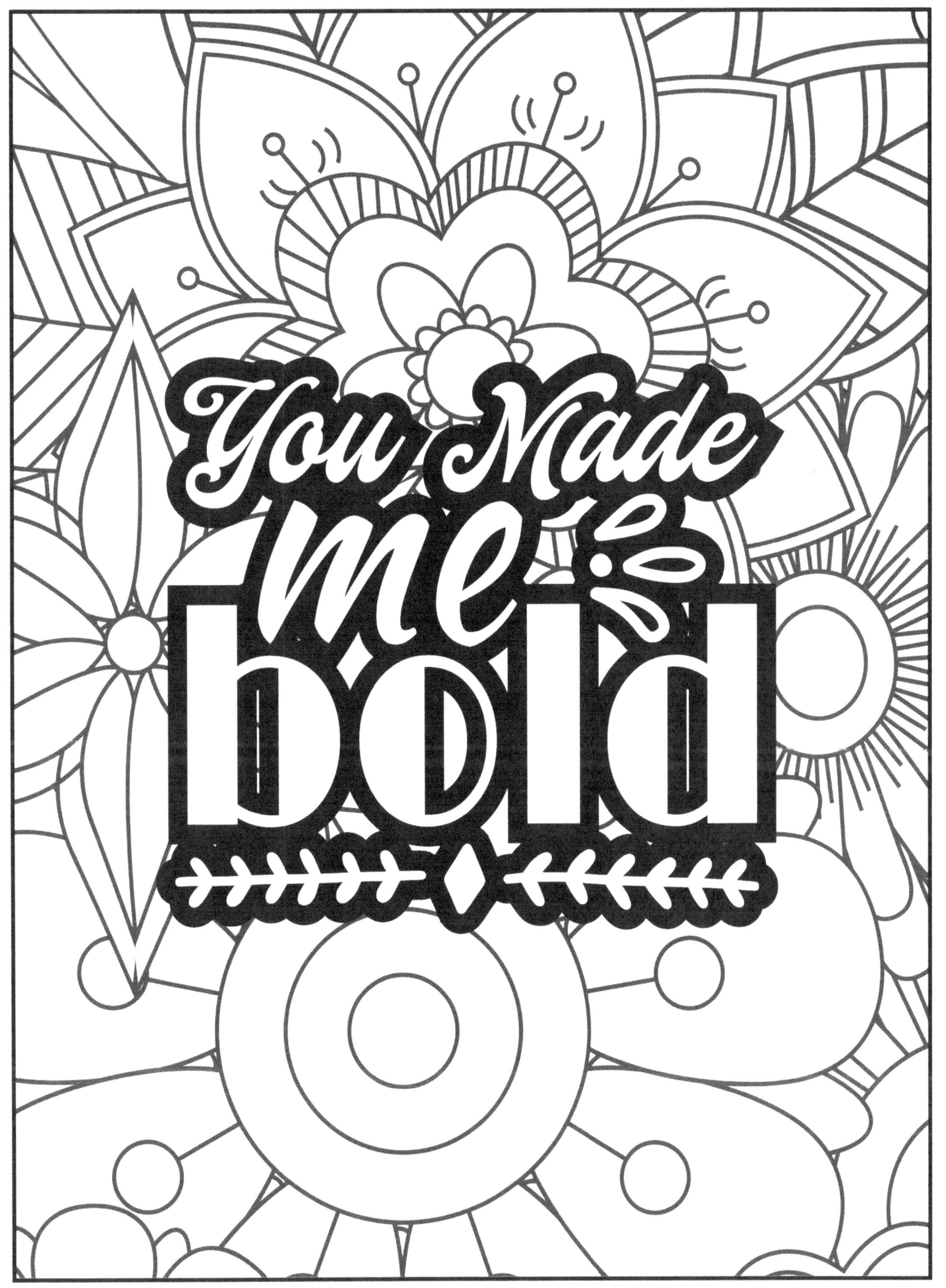

You Made
me
bold

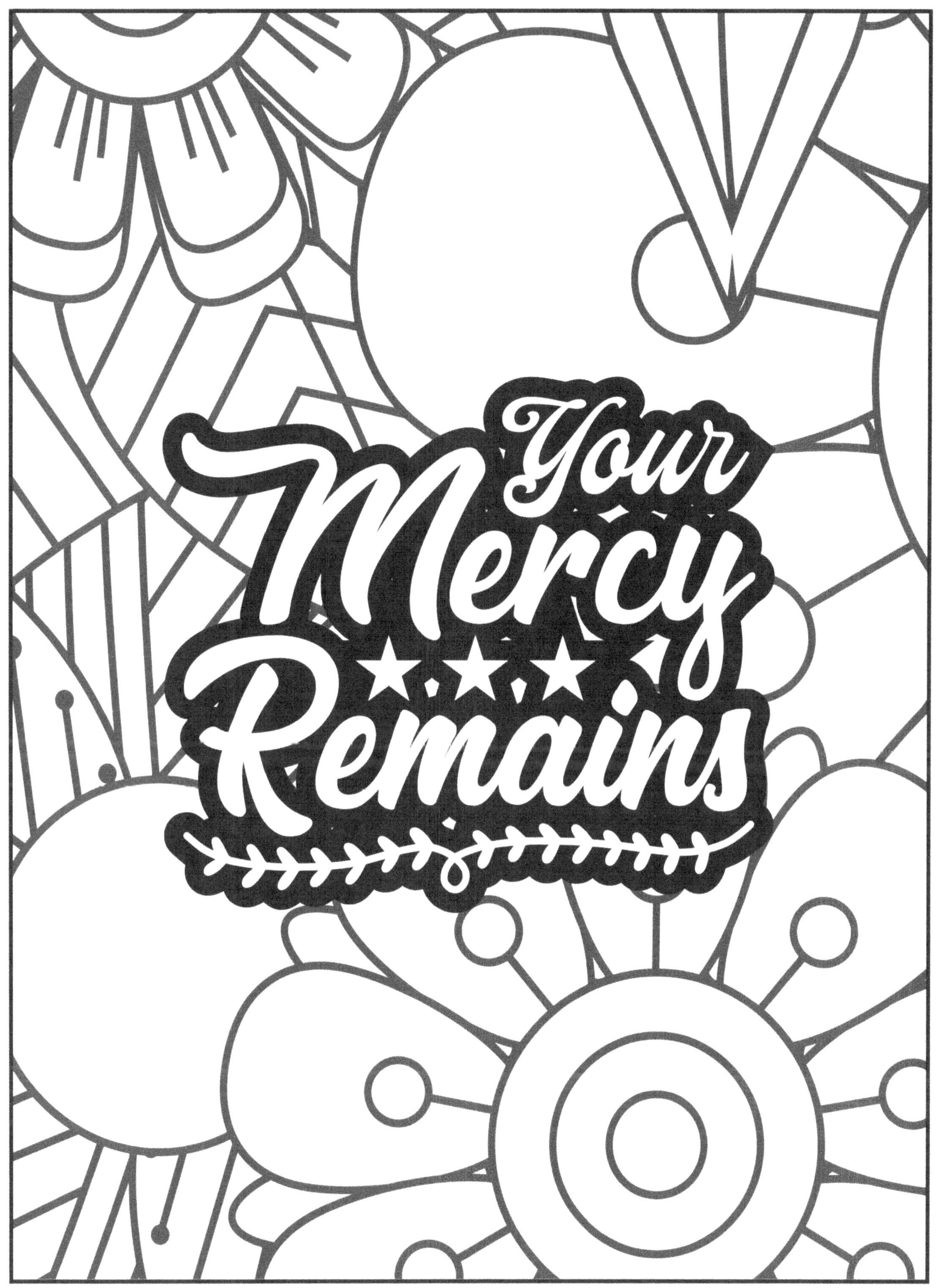

Your
Mercy
Remains

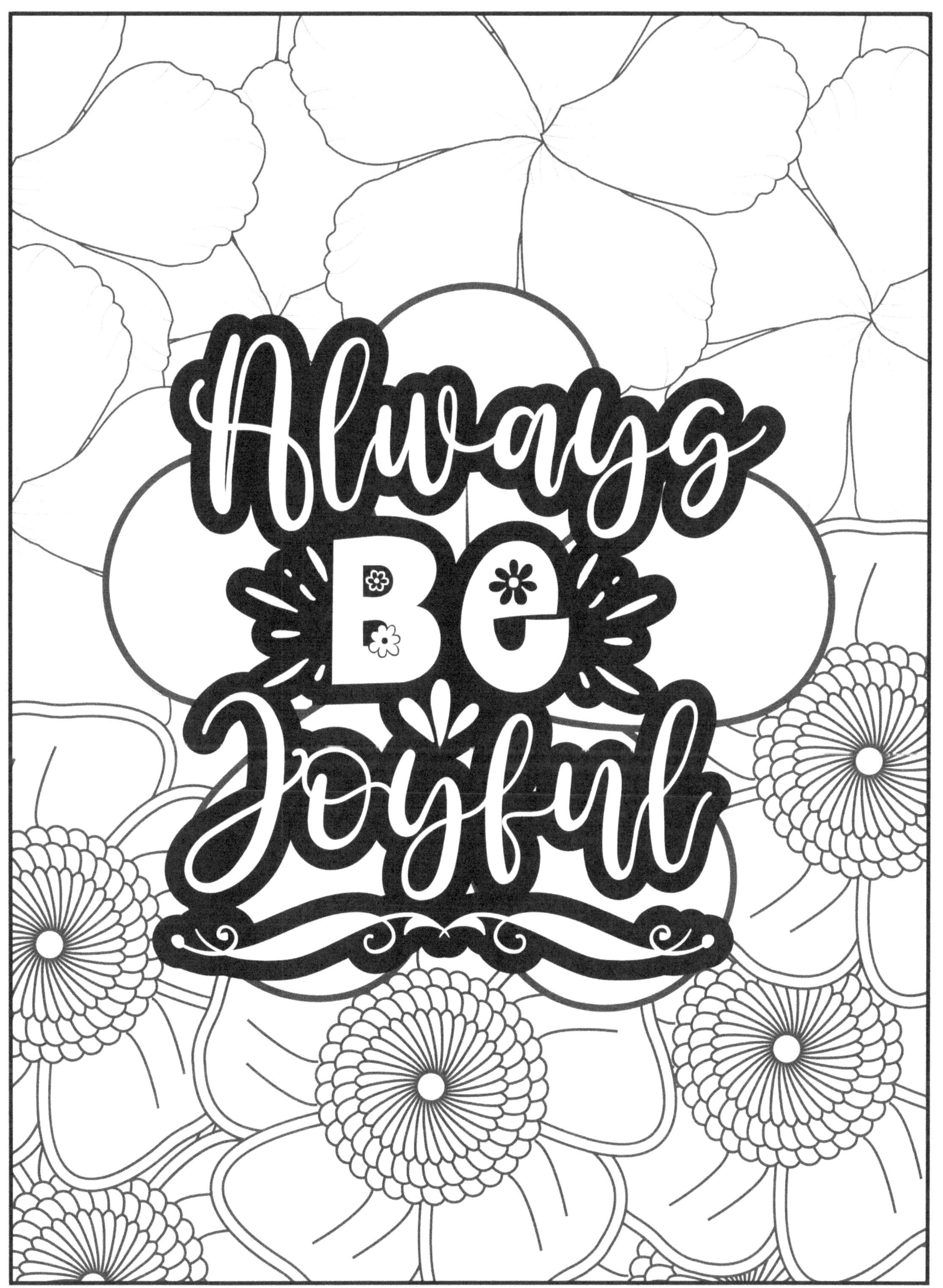

Always
Be
Joyful

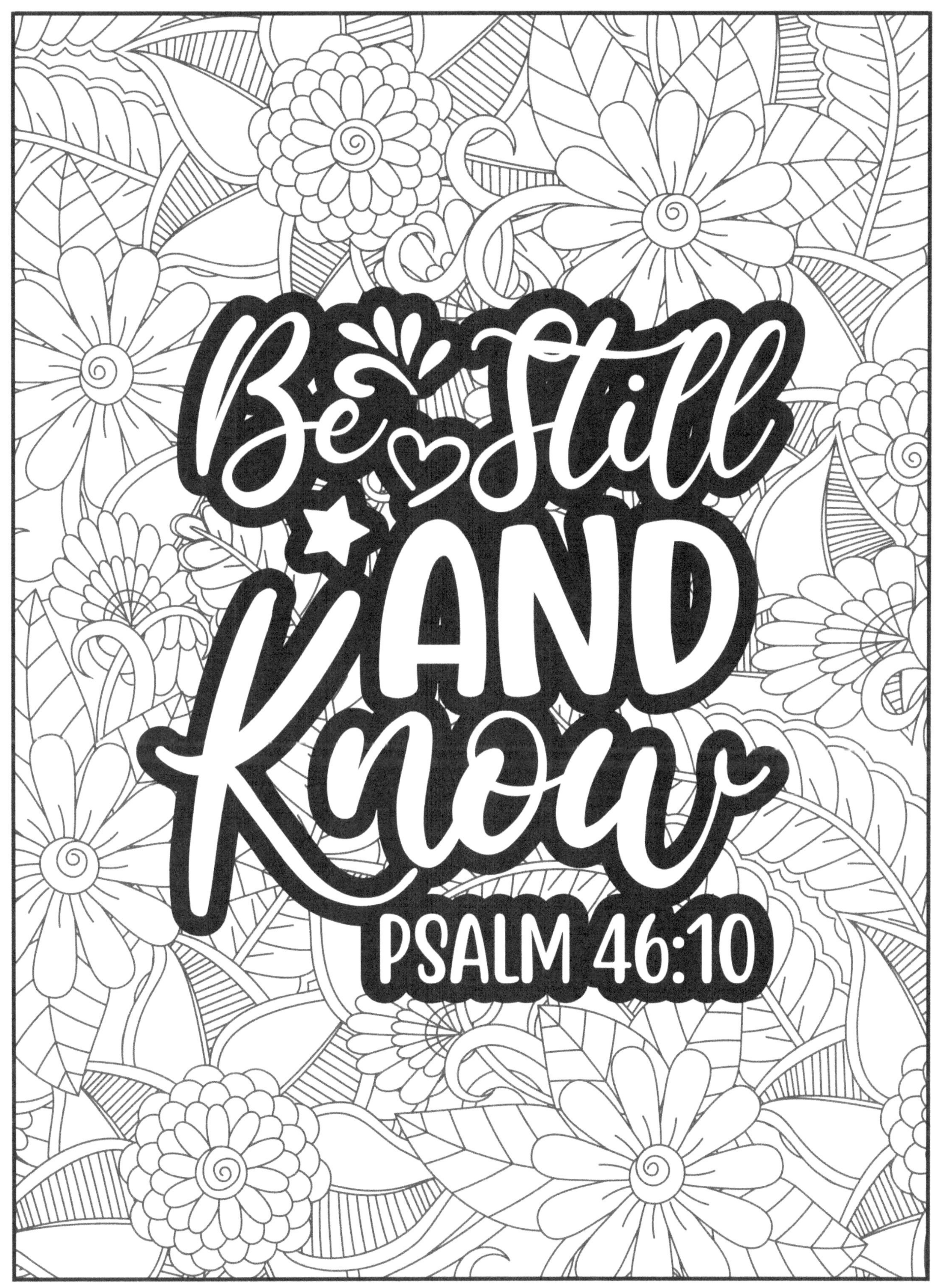
Be Still
AND
Know
PSALM 46:10

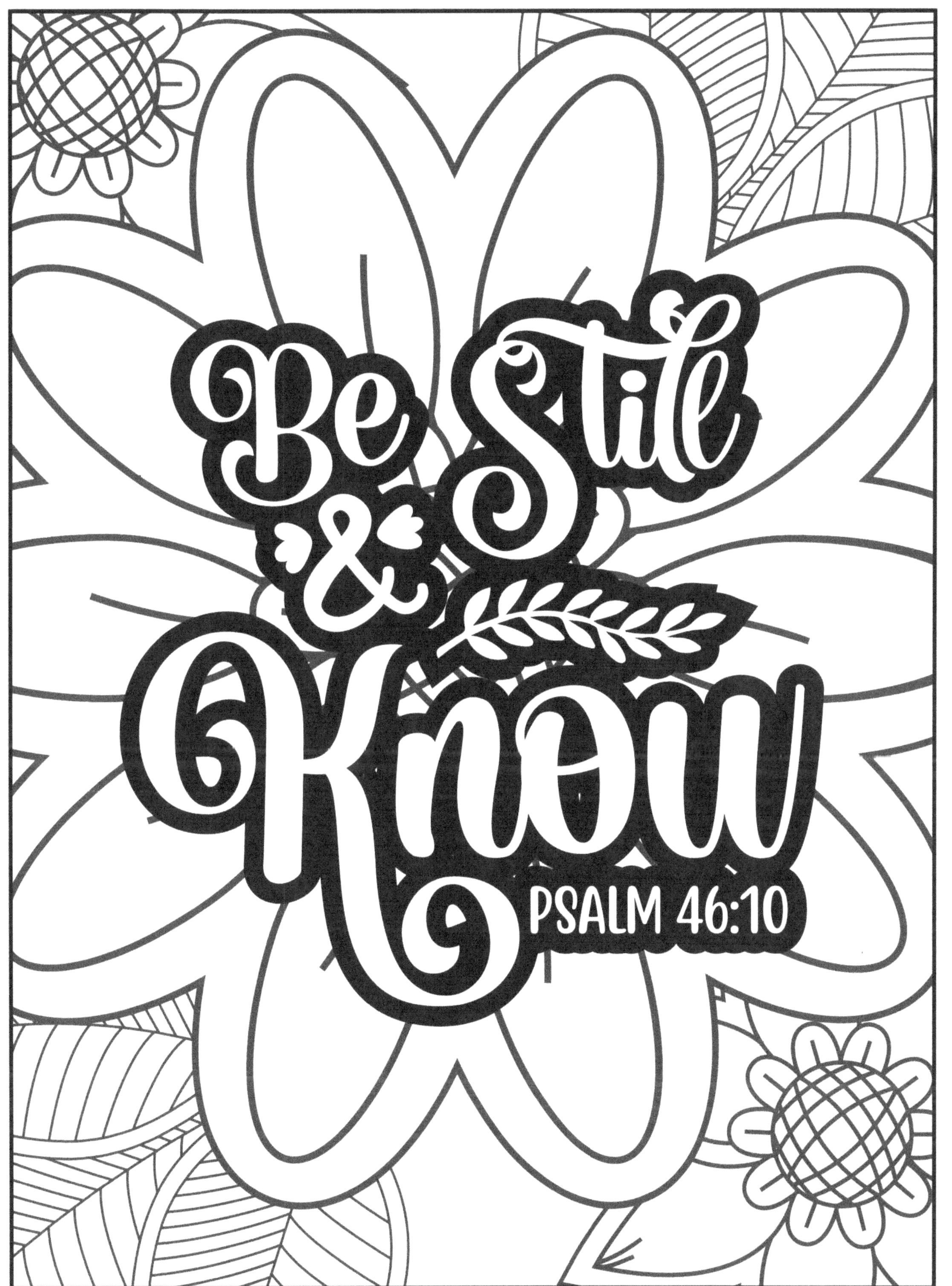

Be Still & Know
PSALM 46:10

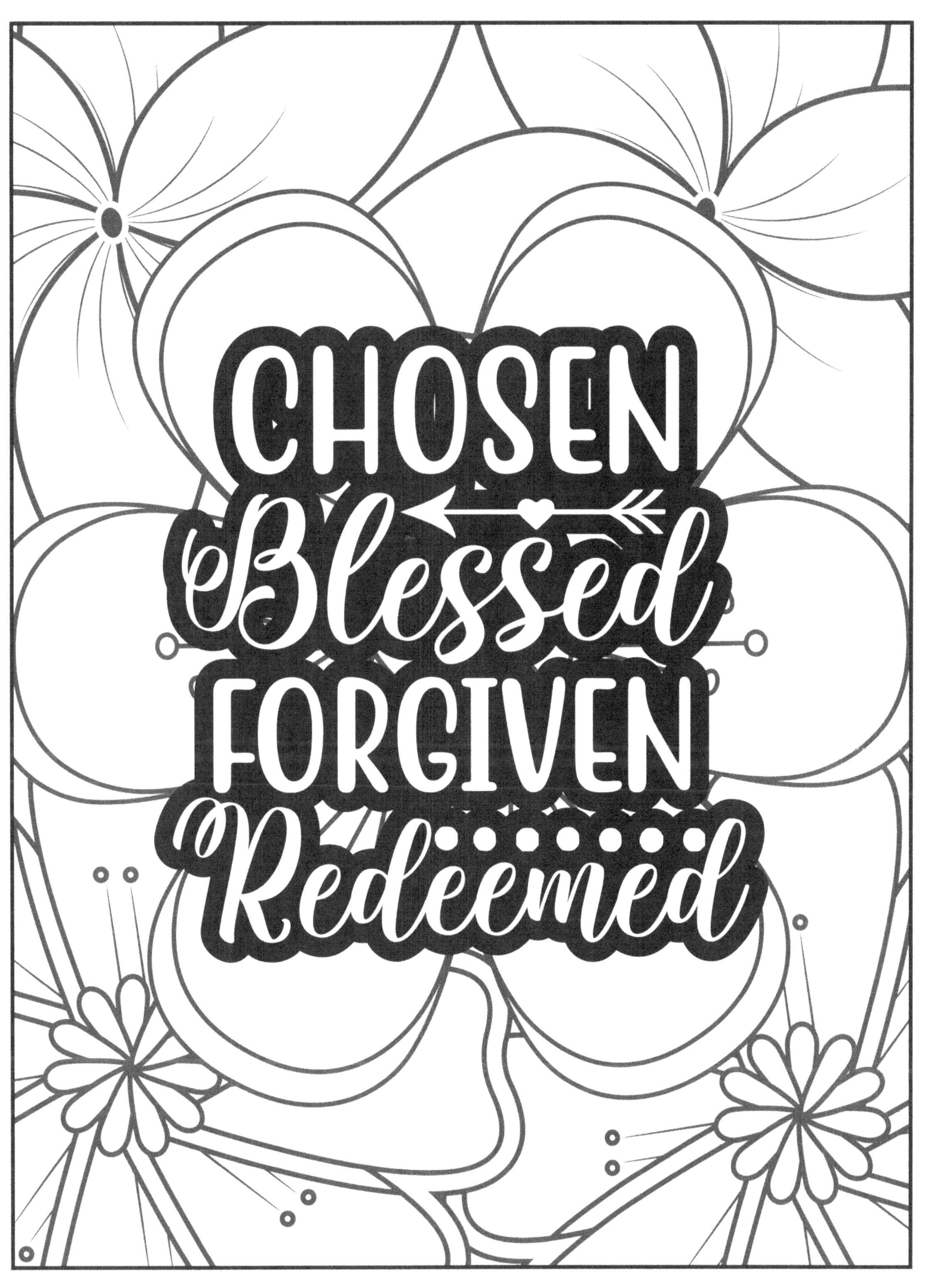

CHOSEN
Blessed
FORGIVEN
Redeemed

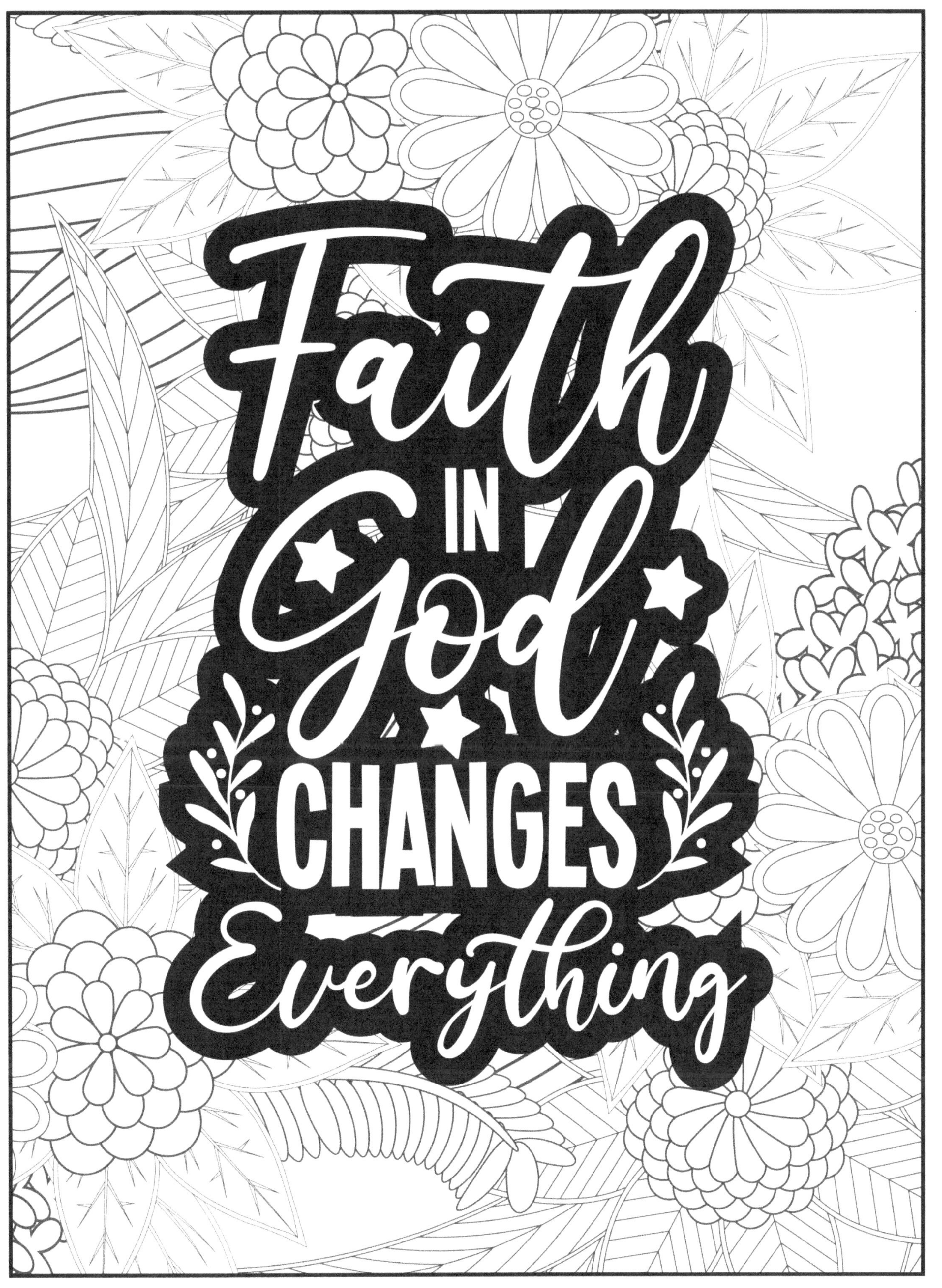
Faith
in
God
Changes
Everything

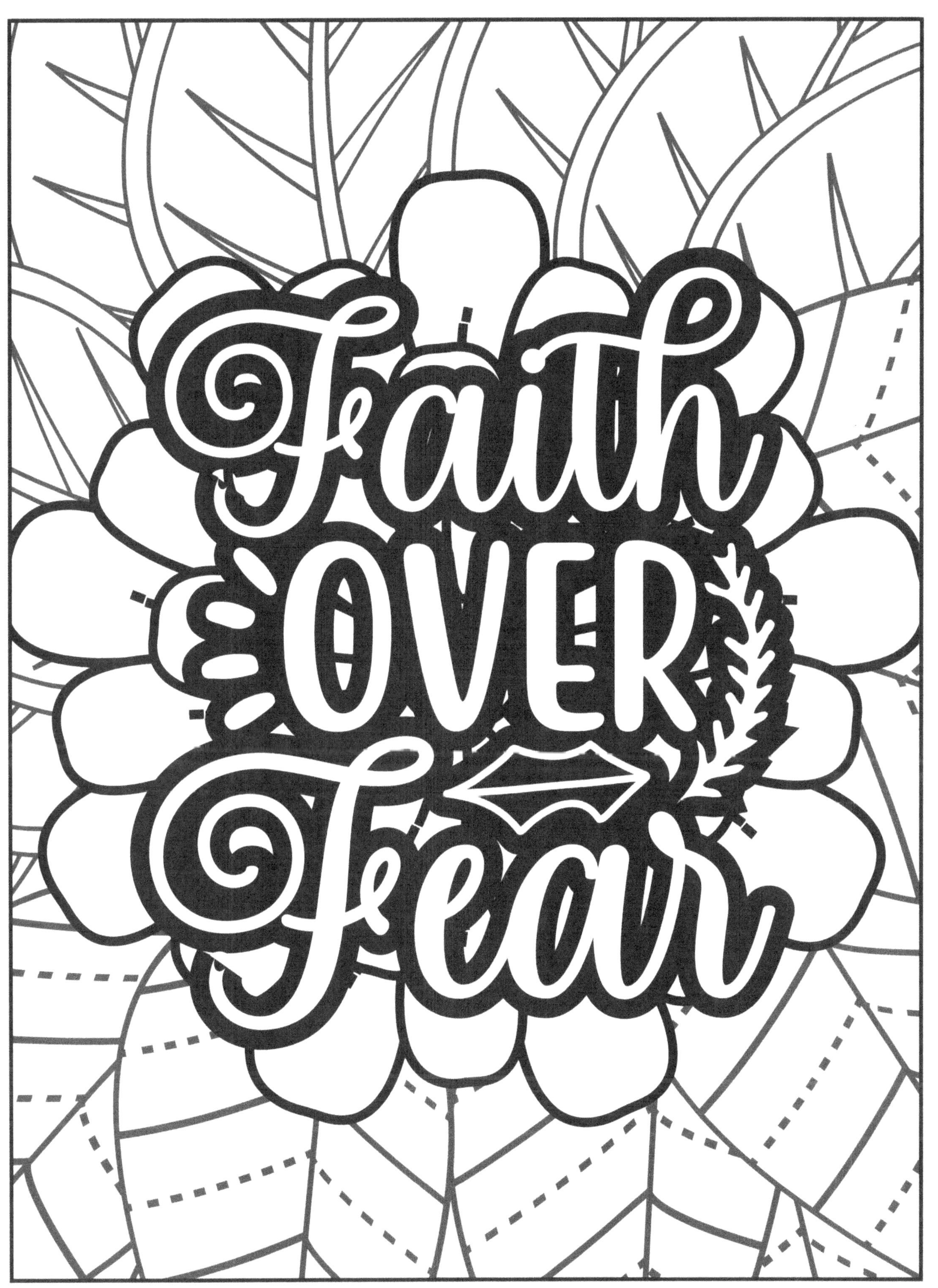

Faith
OVER
Fear

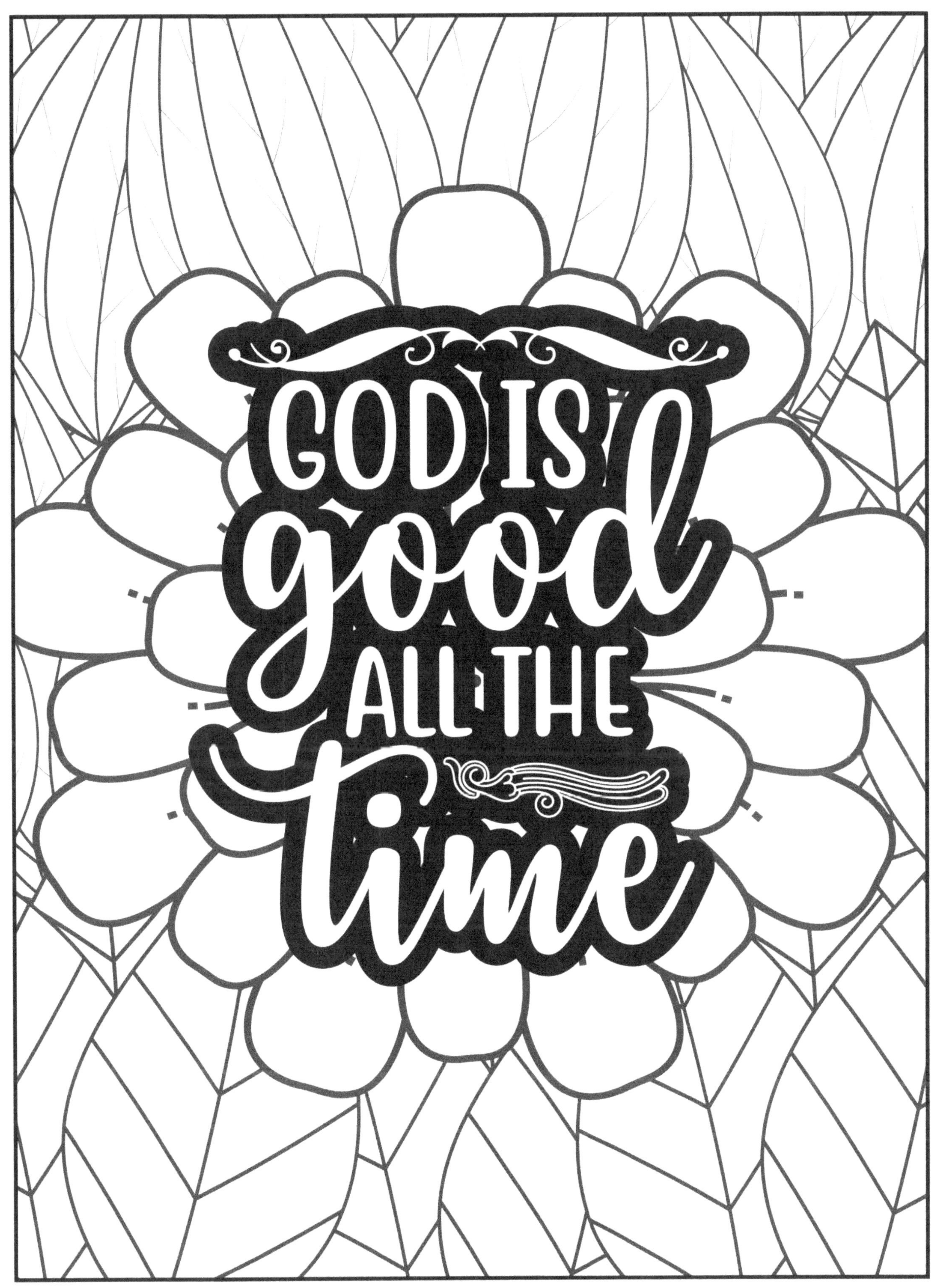

GOD IS
good
ALL THE
time

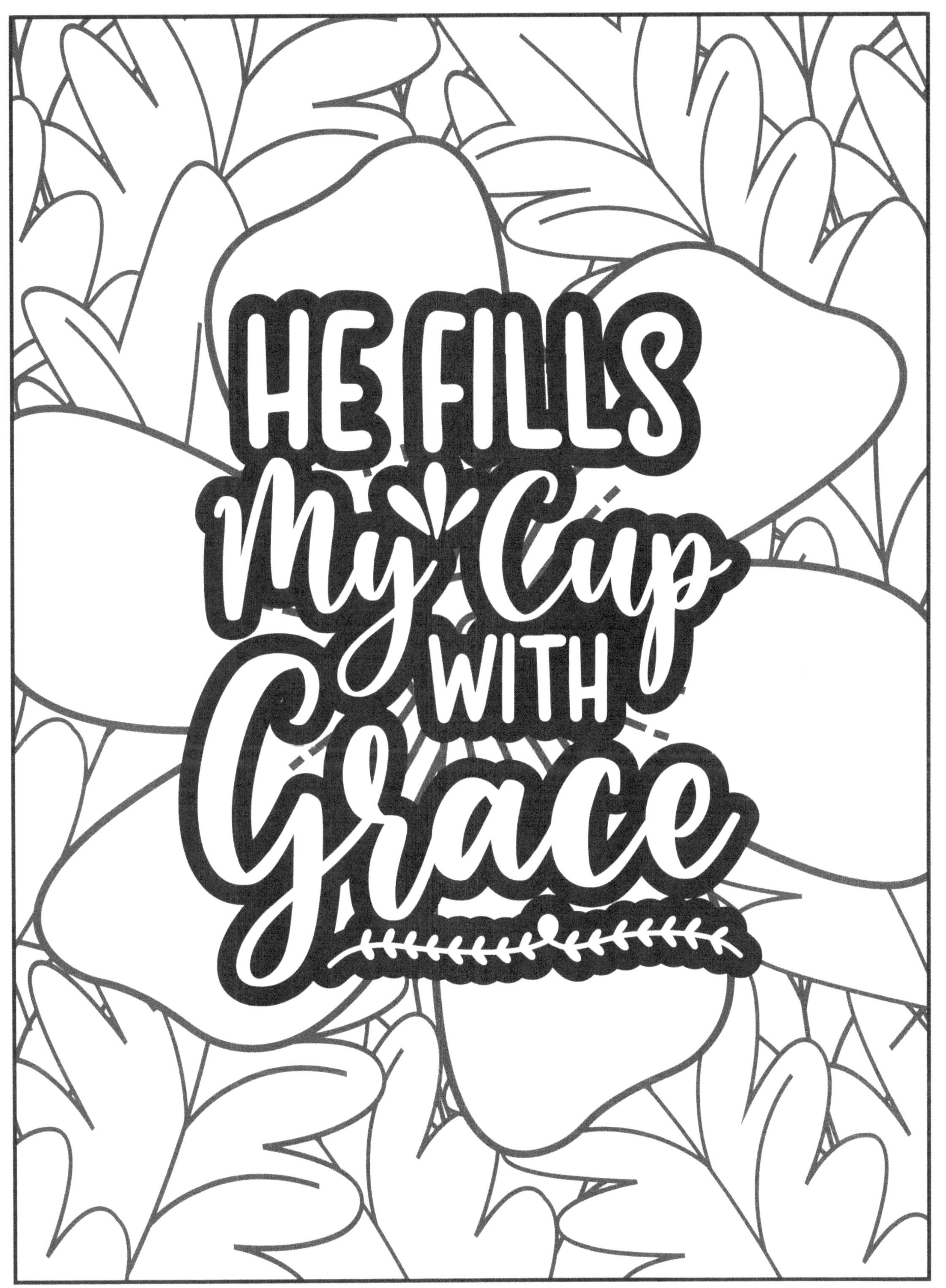

HE FILLS
MY CUP
WITH
Grace

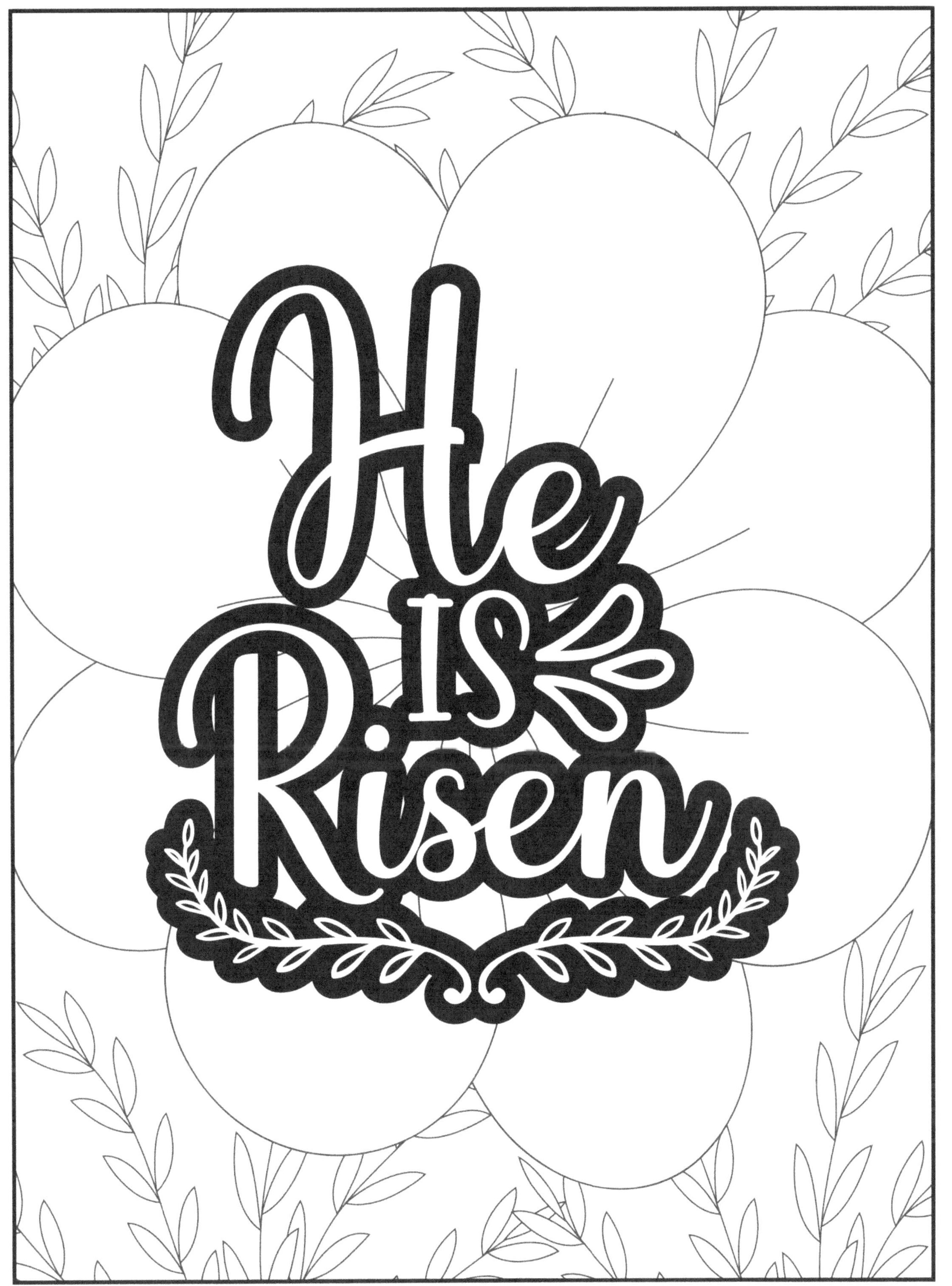

He
is
Risen

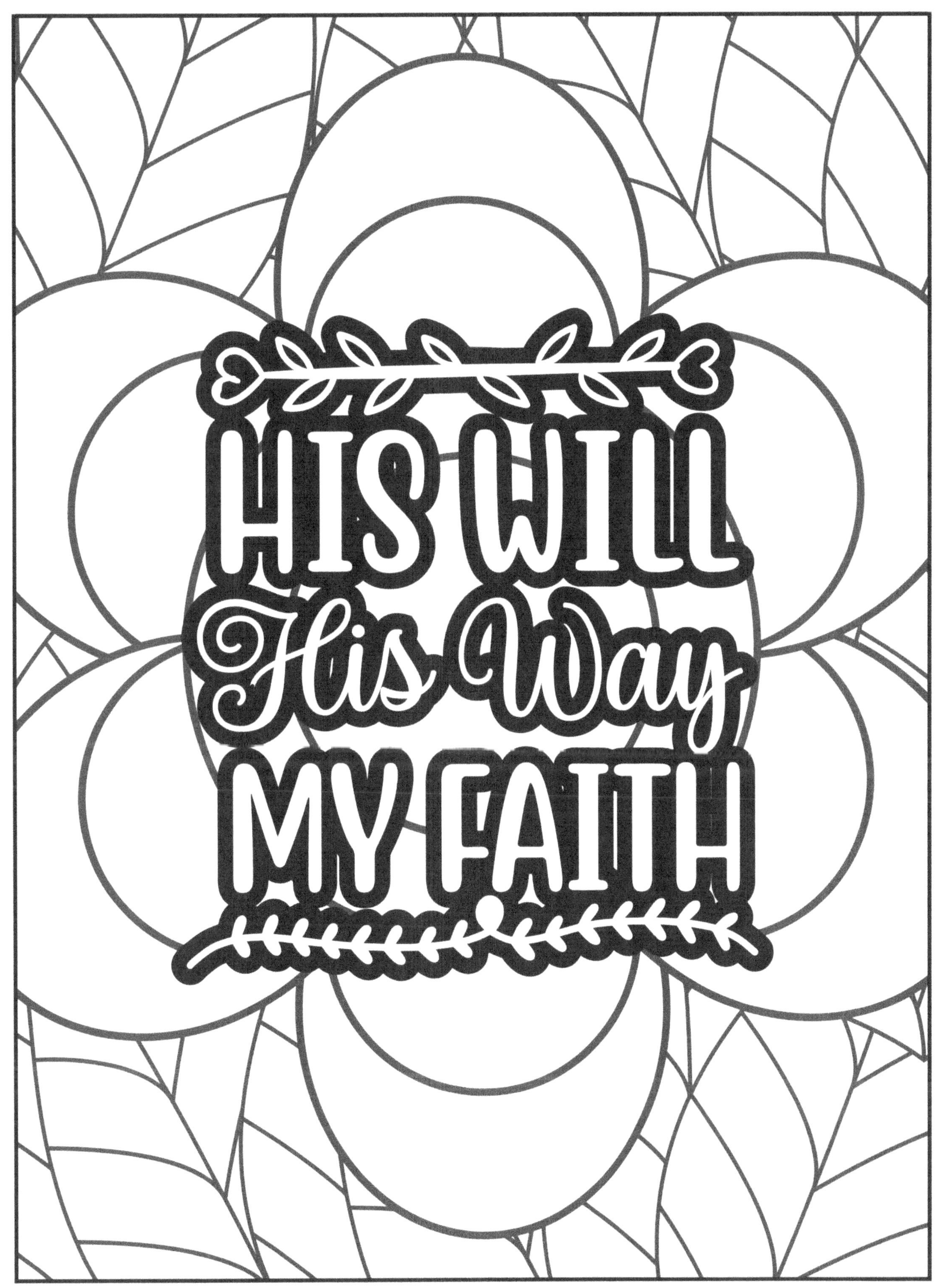

HIS WILL
His Way
MY FAITH

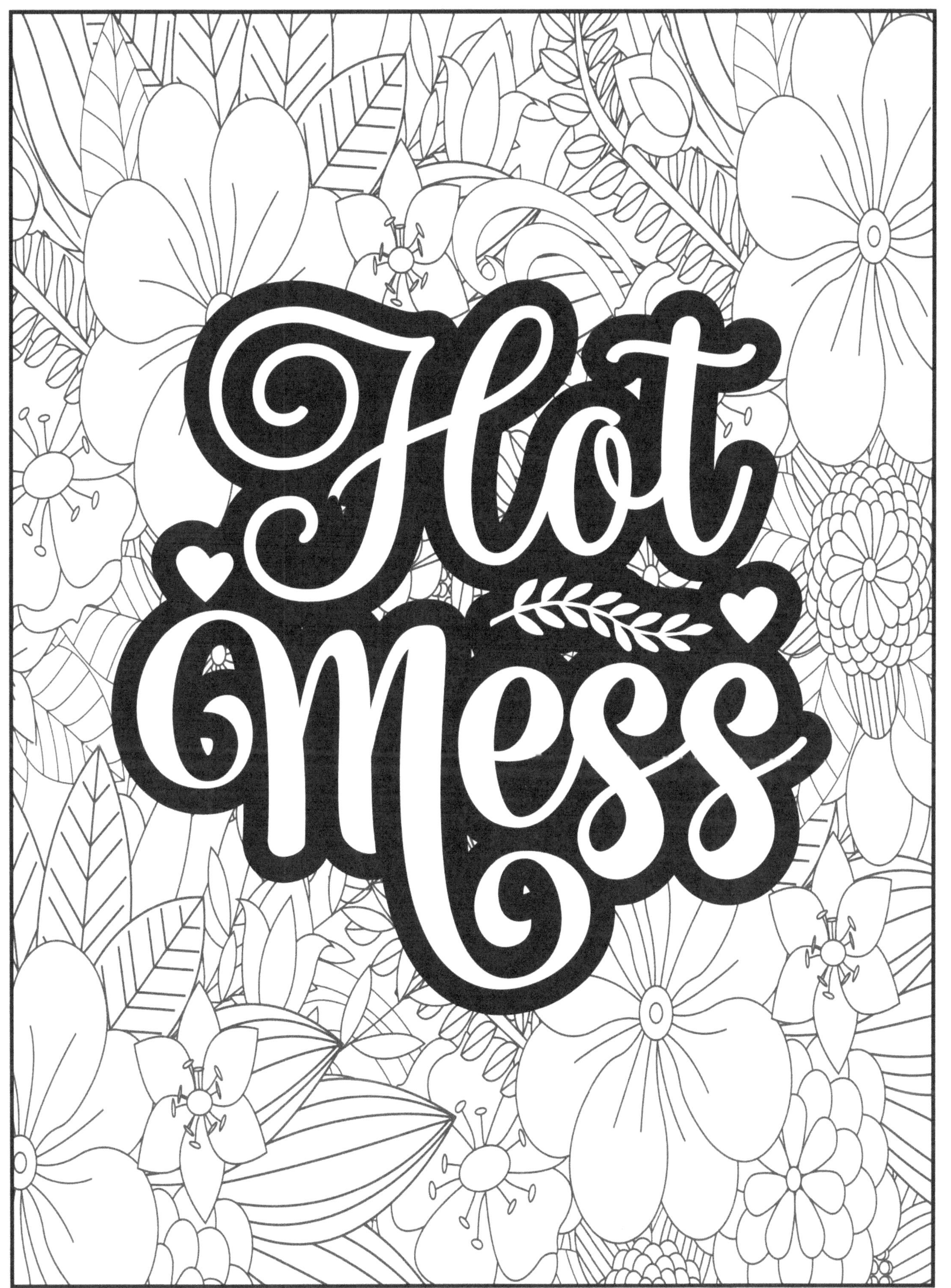
Hot
Mess

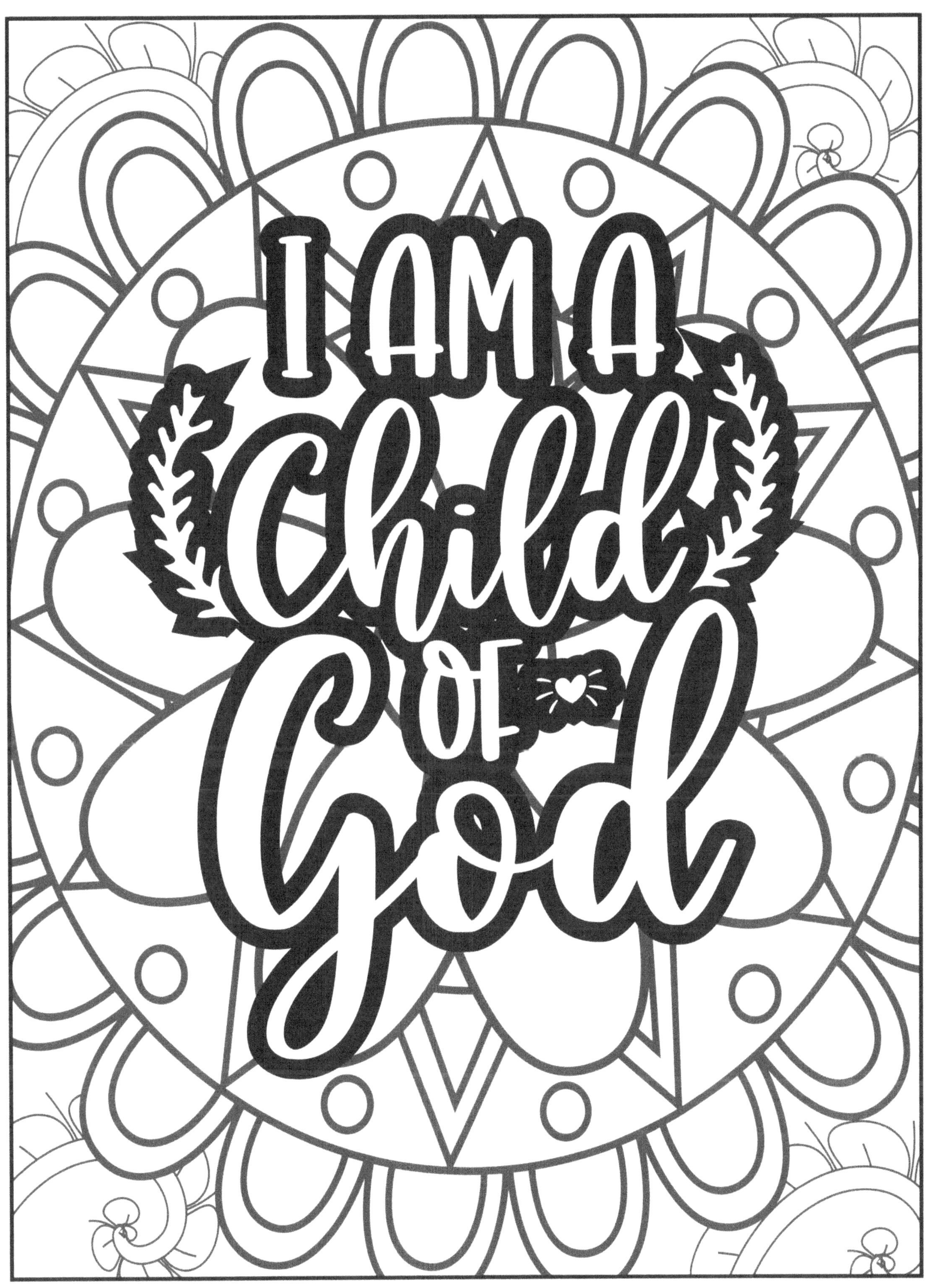

I AM A
Child
OF
God

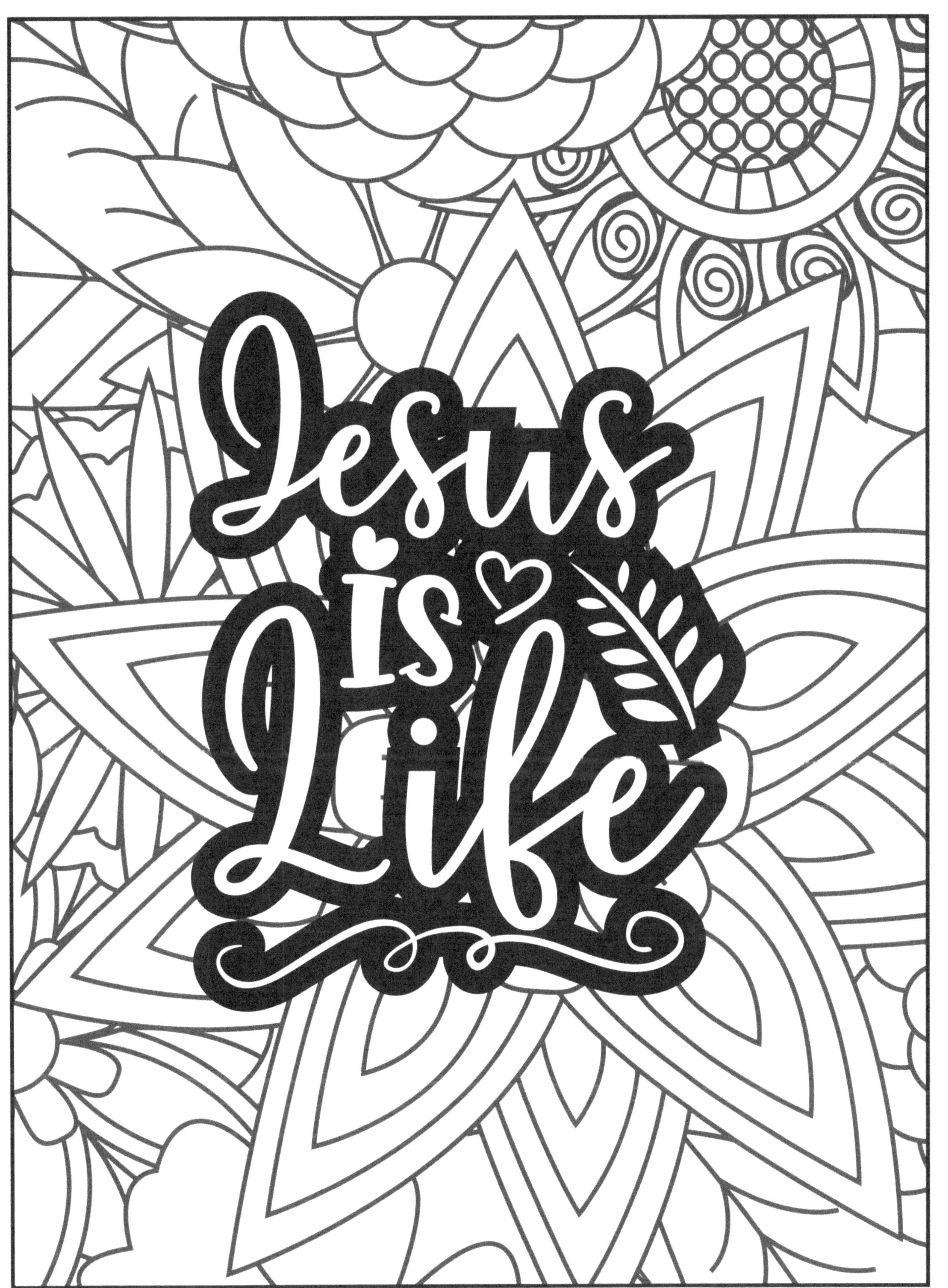
Jesus
is
Life

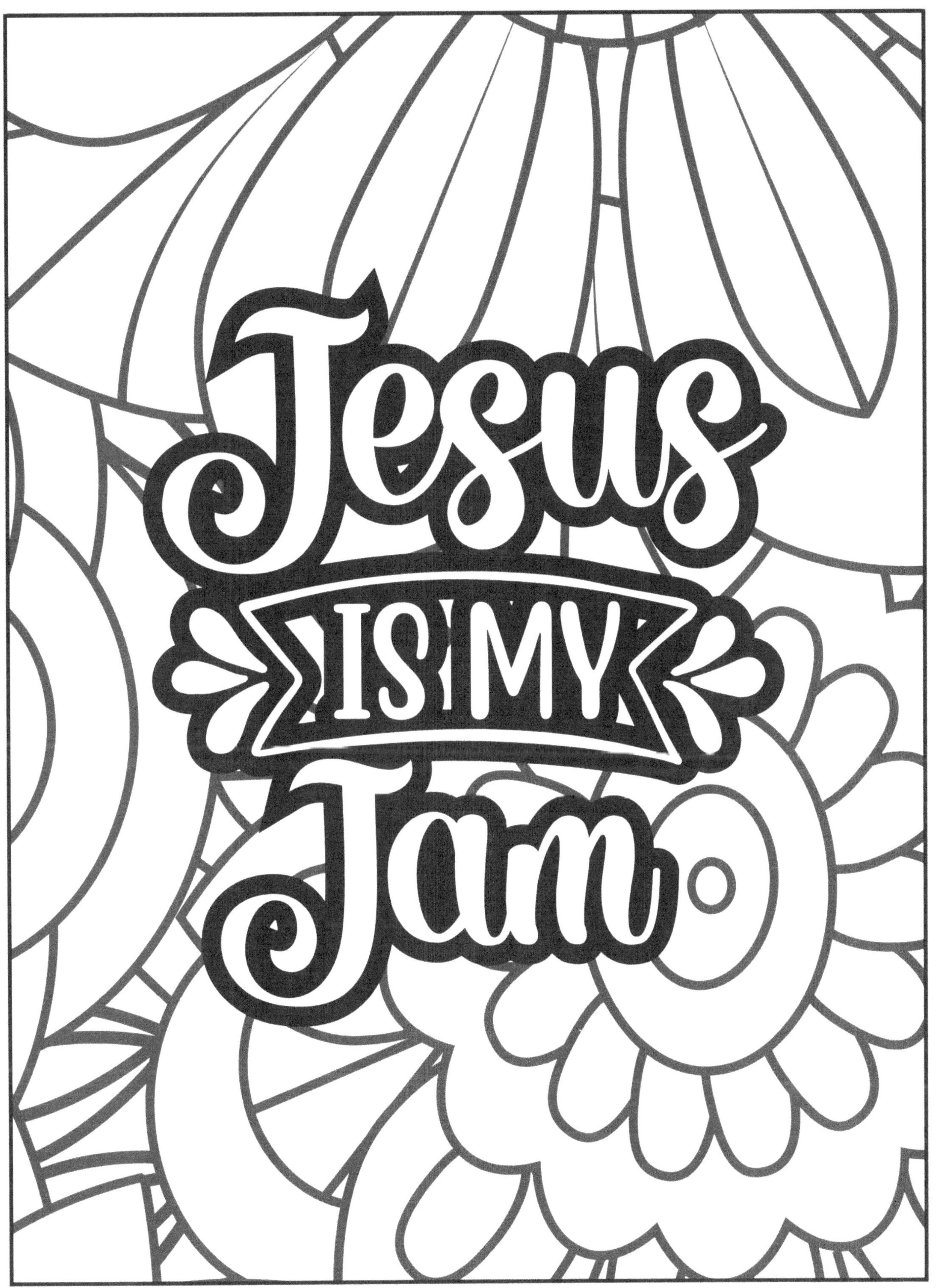

Jesus
IS MY
Jam

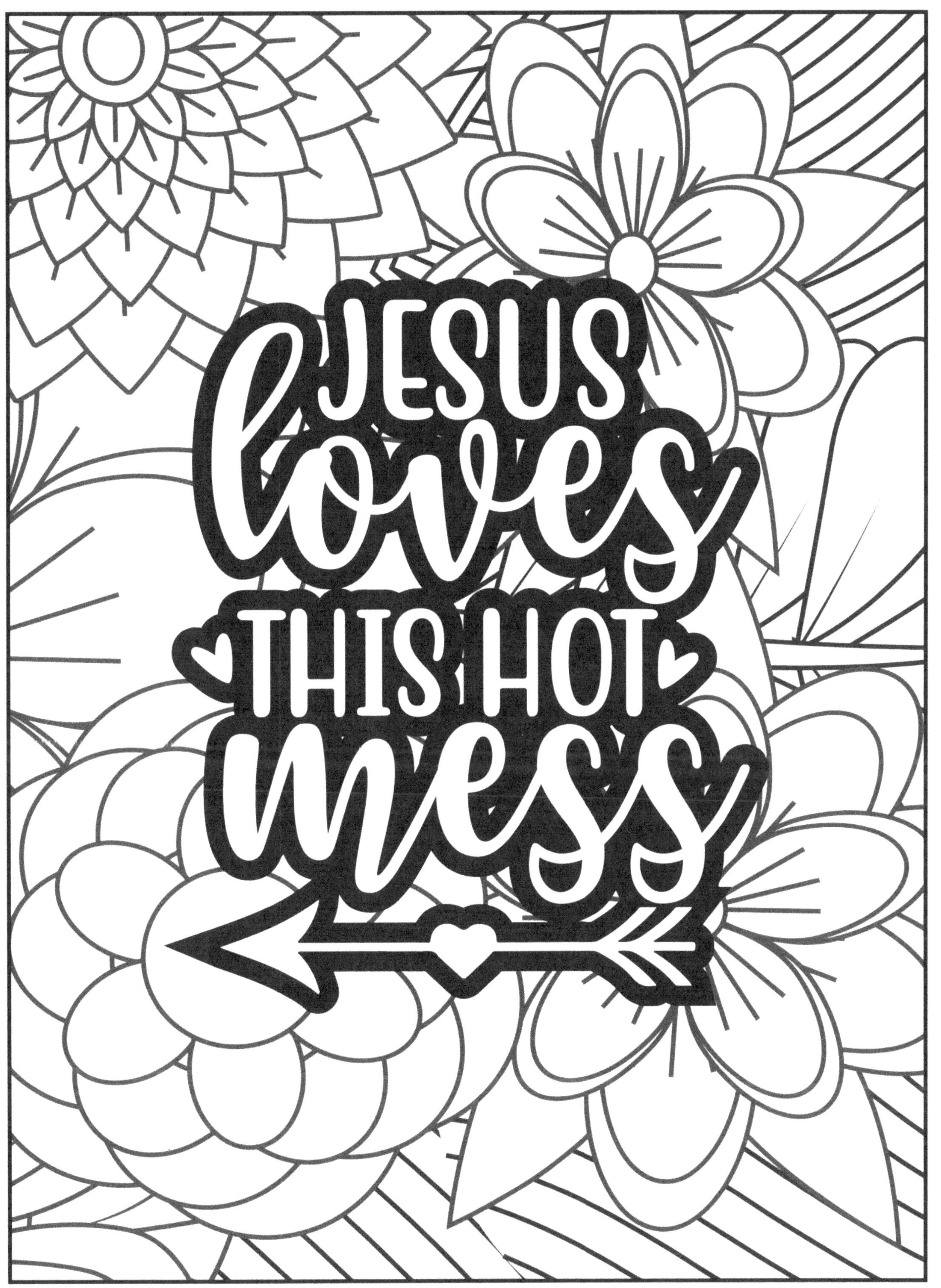

JESUS
loves
THIS HOT
mess

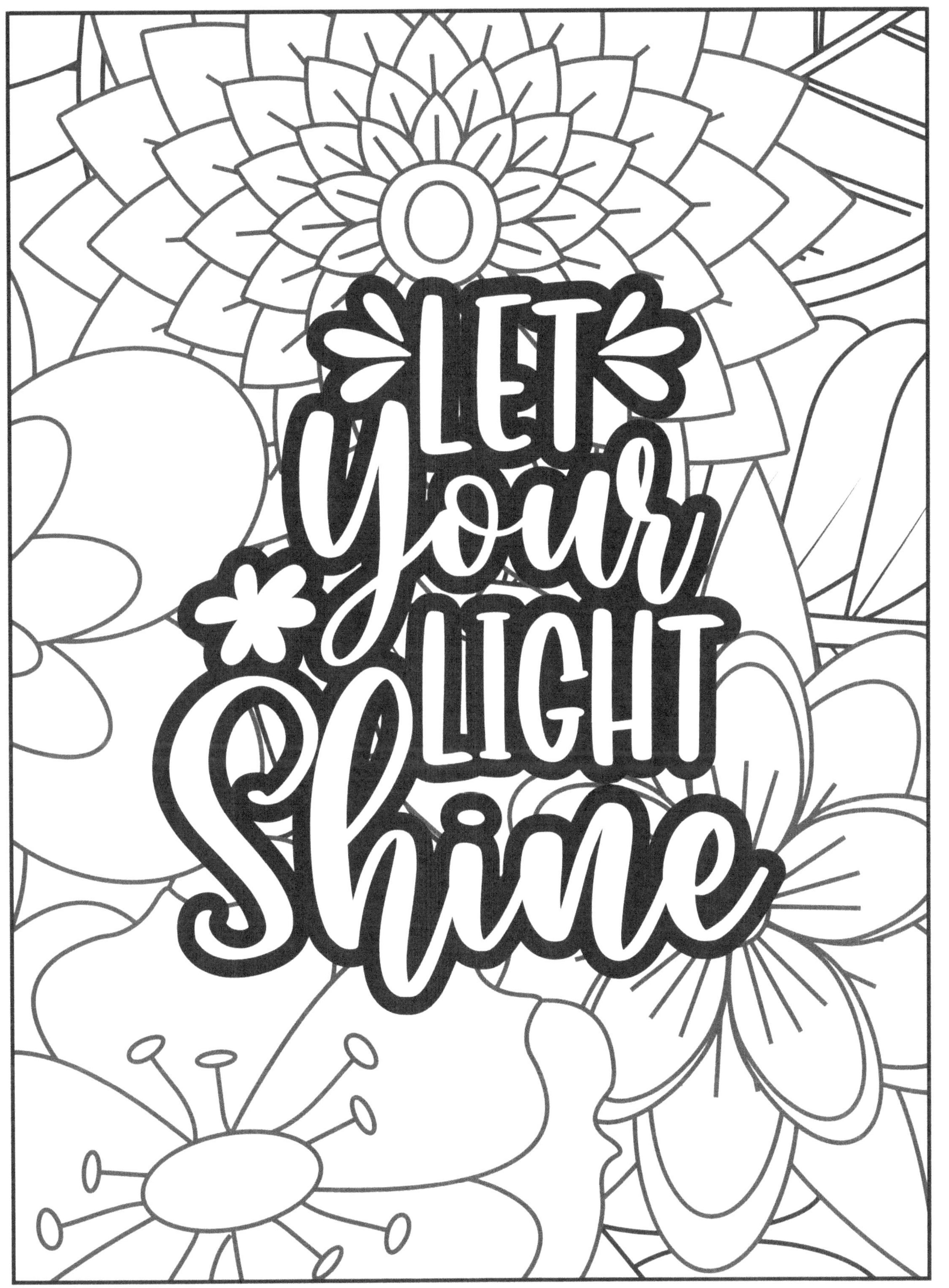

LET
Your
LIGHT
Shine

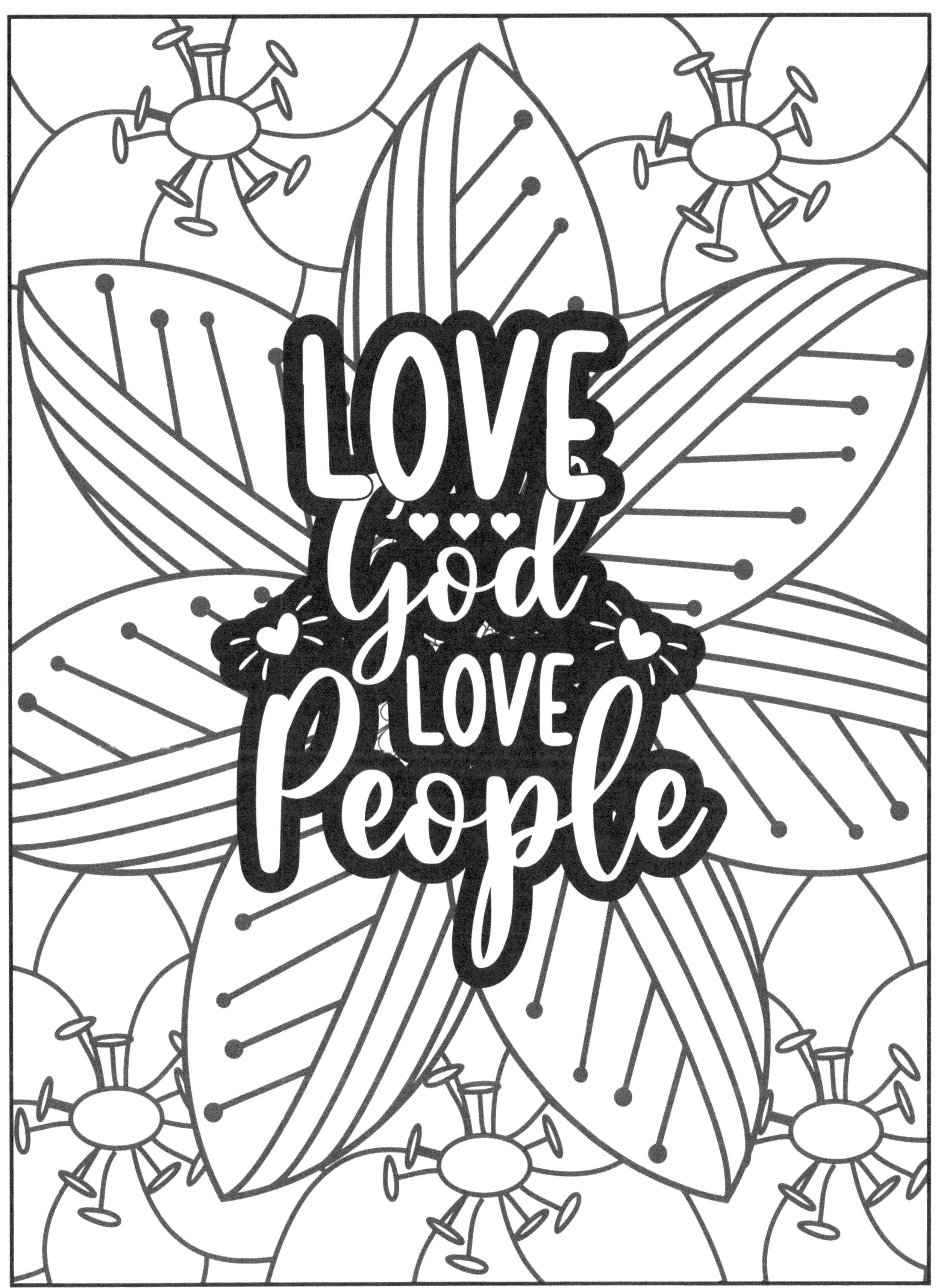

LOVE
God
LOVE
People

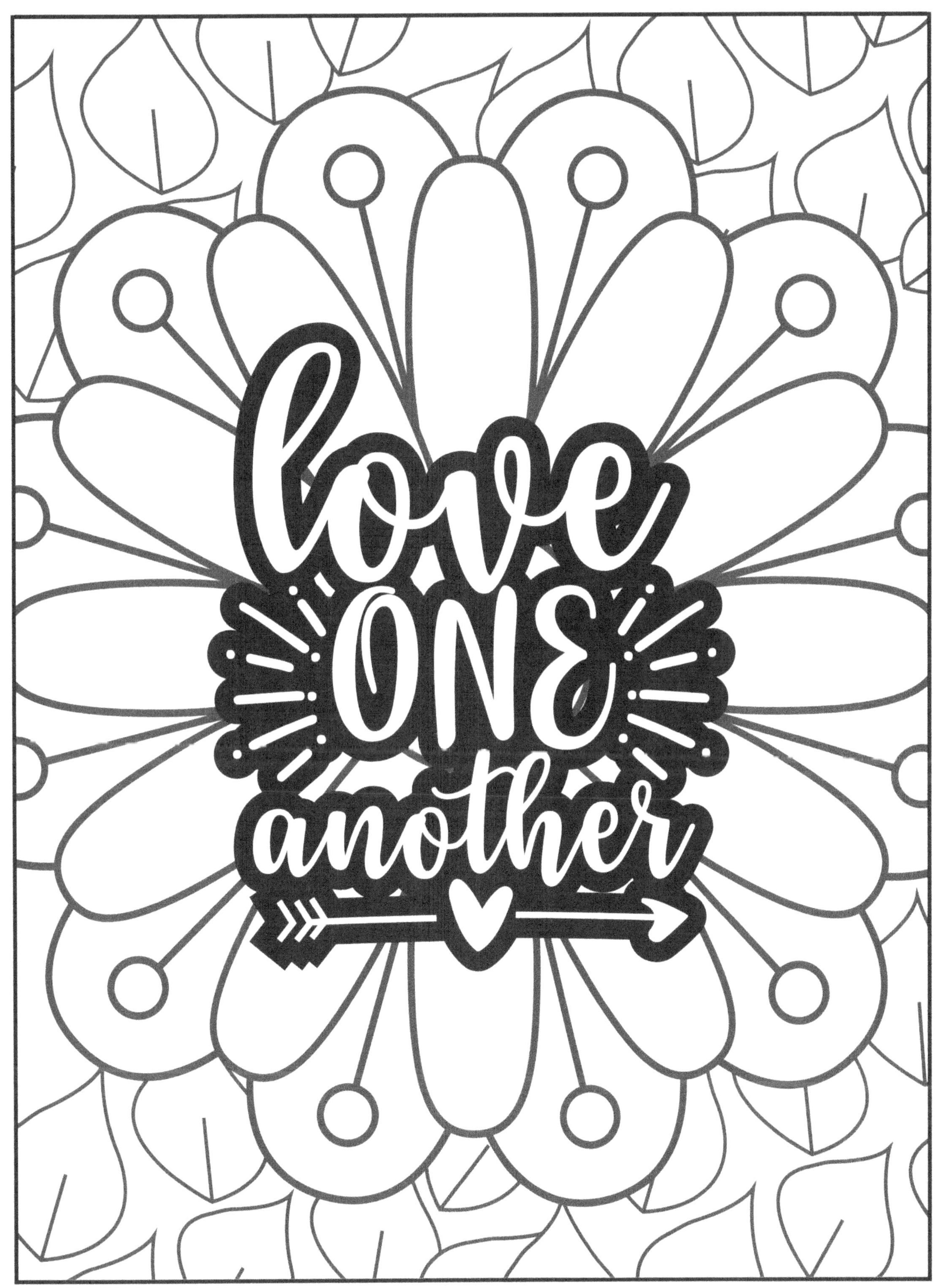

love
ONE
another

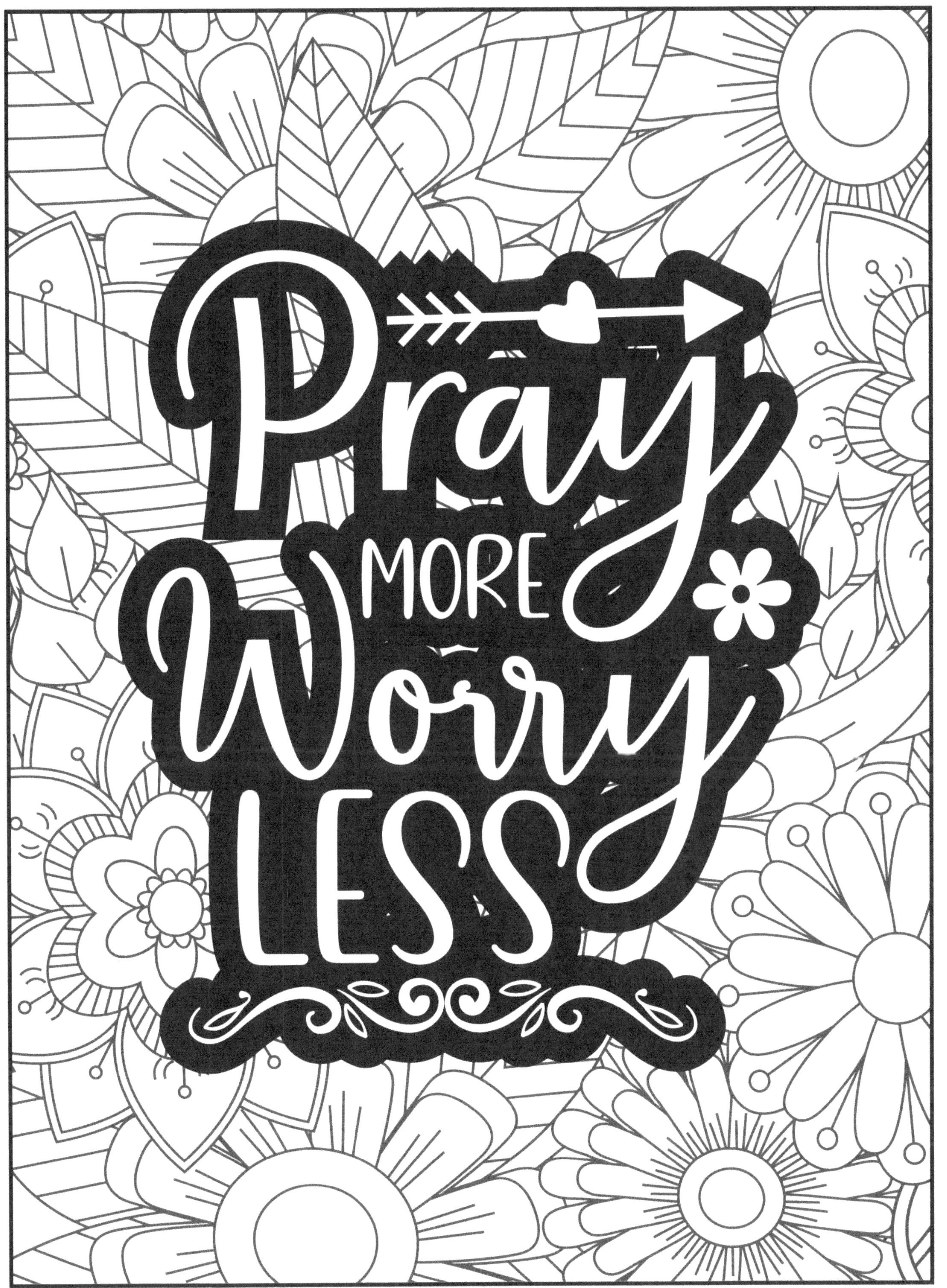

Pray
MORE
Worry
LESS

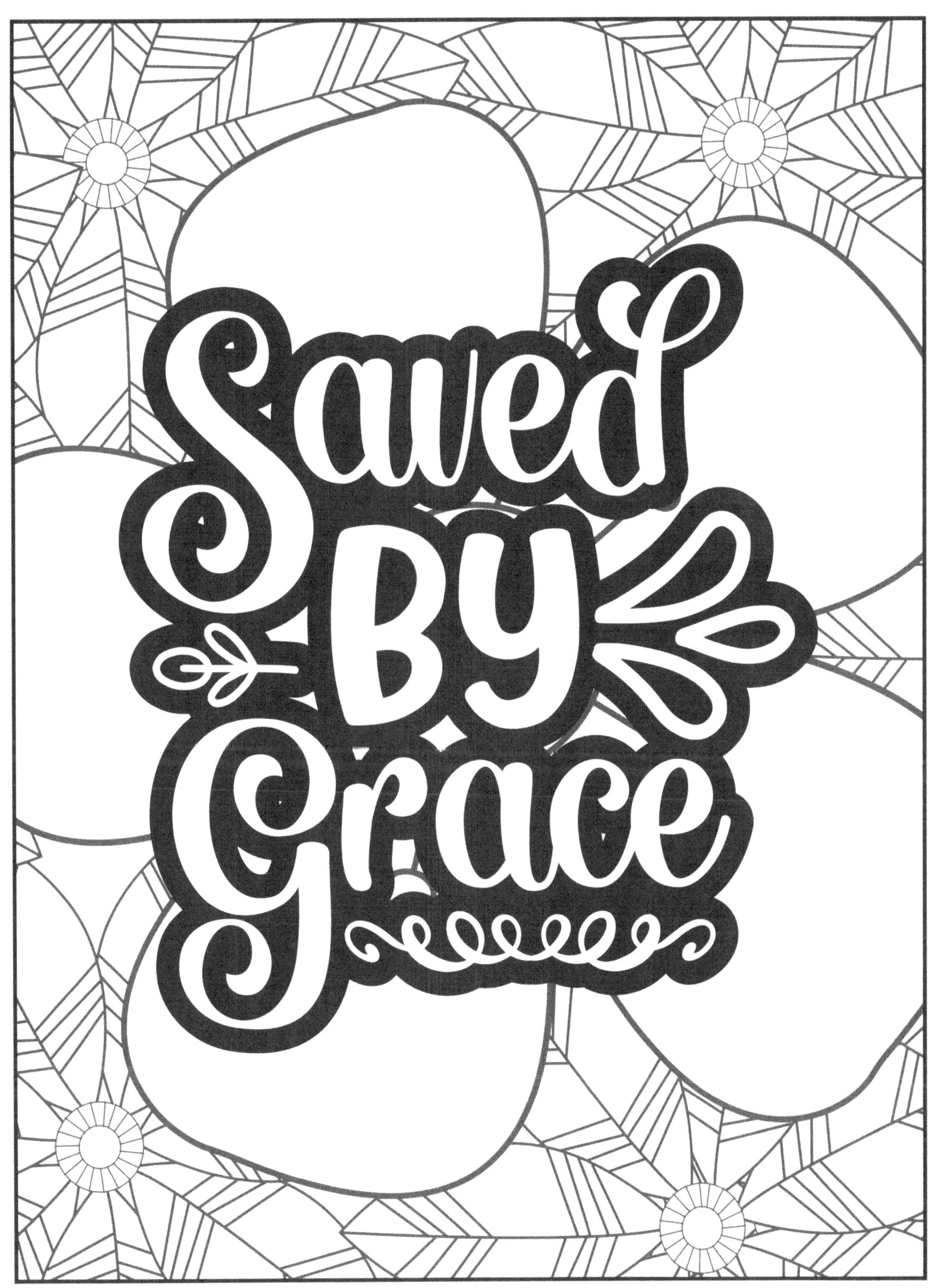

Saved
By
Grace